Larry Thompson
(814) 873-6696

bounce

Miramax Presents

a Steve Golin and Michael Besman Production

a Don Roos Film

Starring

Ben Affleck	David Paymer
Gwyneth Paltrow	Alex D. Linz
Joe Morton	David Dorfman
Natasha Henstridge	Jennifer Grey
Tony Goldwyn	Caroline Aaron
Johnny Galecki	

Casting by
Patrick J. Rush, C.S.A.
Sharon Klein, C.S.A.

Costume Designer
Peter Mitchell

Music Supervisor
Randall Poster

Music by
Mychael Danna

Edited by
David Codron

Production Designer
David Wasco

Director of Photography
Robert Elswit

Co-Producers
Alan C. Blomquist
Bobby Cohen

Executive Producers
Bob Weinstein
Harvey Weinstein
Bob Osher
Meryl Poster

Produced by
Steve Golin
Michael Besman

Written and Directed by
Don Roos

bounce

an original screenplay by

don roos

talk
miramax
books
new york

Copyright © 2000 Don Roos

All rights reserved. No part of this book may be used or reproduced in any manner whatsoever without the written permission of the Publisher. Printed in the United States of America. For information address: Hyperion, 77 W. 66th Street, New York, New York 10023-6298.

Library of Congress Cataloging-in-Publication Data

ISBN: 0-7868-8589-0

FIRST EDITION

10 9 8 7 6 5 4 3 2 1

fade in:
ext. chicago skyline (aerial)—day

Skyscrapers poking into clouds. A late afternoon in December.

ext. chicago street—day

A guy in his early thirties waits with a small group outside a Holiday Inn by the interstate for the shuttle to take him to the airport. He looks at the sky anxiously: snow? He checks his watch and as he looks up, he sees a limo pass him.

the guy's pov—the limo

Eases onto I-90.

ext. i-90 west to o'hare airport, chicago, illinois— day

Snow is starting to stick to the roadway now. A MAN by a stuck car is flagging down a tow truck. We PICK OUT one car, a limousine, and then ONE VOICE, casual, somewhere between contented and smug:

> BUDDY'S VOICE
> What do you think happened?... You're kidding me. That's what you think happened? You really think that?

int. limo—(moving)—day

BUDDY AMARAL, early thirties, is on a cell phone. He's drinking but not drunk, not what he would call drunk. As a result of a lifetime of things going his way, Buddy's a happy guy. His deals always close, his girlfriends always open; he will never be audited. Lucky. With him it's fifty-fifty at best: there's a decent guy inside, but it's hard to hate him. If you're a woman he's like your kid brother, the total pain who sometimes says, "You look nice in that dress." If you're a guy, he's your second pick for any team. Not your first, because you don't want him to think you need him. But second, because he'll fight like hell and pretend to not notice your fumbles.

BUDDY

(into phone)
You scare too easy, you know that, Jim? You're like . . .
I don't know. Someone who scares too easy. He loves us.
He fucking loves us.

As he talks, Buddy changes out of his dress shirt into a sweater; he kicks off his shoes, slips on loafers . . .

BUDDY

You want a quote? "I can't see why we would ever leave."
He had tears in his voice; I thought he was gonna give me a corsage. I got the signed contract right here.

On the seat next to him is a stack of documents. We see the Infinity Air logo on the stationery; it's also on the luggage tags on Buddy's luggage.

BUDDY

I'm on their six o'clock flight—I'm comped for life, I'm telling you, they would've put me in the fucking cockpit but the seats are smaller and there's no movie. Anyway, I'll see you tomorrow morning, okay? Hey. My pleasure. You, too.

ext. o'hare airport—day

Almost dusk. The snow plows are now out in force.

int. o'hare—infinity terminal—night

The departures board: two Infinity flights to Los Angeles are listed. The 4:00 P.M. reads CANCELED; *the 6:00 P.M. (Flight 82) reads* DELAYED. *There's a long line at the check-in desk and the waiting area's packed. We HEAR an announcement:*

> ANNOUNCER (V.O.)
> *(over P.A. system)*
> Would those passengers confirmed on Flight 82 to Los Angeles willing to accept travel vouchers for a later flight please make themselves known to any Infinity employee? Thank you.

Buddy is standing by another businessman, RON WACHTER, a friendly late-forties guy. They both squint up at the departures board.

> BUDDY
>
> Shit.

> WACHTER
>
> O'Hare. Hell with runways and a coupla TCBYs. L.A.?

> BUDDY
>
> Shows, huh?

> WACHTER
>
> Think I flew out with you Tuesday morning. Ron Wachter.

> BUDDY
> *(didn't notice him)*
> Buddy Amaral. Well, we'll get out. I've seen it worse.

Behind him:

JANICE

Hey, Buddy. You made it out.

Buddy turns, sees JANICE GUERRERO, an Infinity employee.

BUDDY

Janice. I was gonna call you.

JANICE

I was gonna hold my breath.

Wachter smiles: to be thirty again. He goes off.

JANICE

Did we like your dog and pony show?

BUDDY

What can I say? Love at first sight.

JANICE

Lucky us. You on the six? We're just about to push it back.

BUDDY

Fuck. Got time for a drink?

JANICE

That's why they called me in on my day off. Drinks with the freight.

BUDDY

(makes a telephone with his hand)
Next time.

Janice knows what Buddy's like. Maybe it bothered her once. Not now: she smiles, lifts her hand up, too, flips him off. Buddy smiles, heads down the terminal.

ext. o'hare—runways—night

Plows trying to keep up with the snow . . .

int. o'hare—infinity gate area—bar—night

Buddy's got two drinks in his hand, aiming for one of those tall bar tables where MIMI, a businesswoman, attractive, in her thirties, waits for him. The floodlights outside show the driving white snow. That, and the crowds, tell us that O'Hare is struggling to stay open.

Just as he gets to the table Buddy's bumped from behind by GREG JANELLO, the guy we saw back in town, waiting for his airport shuttle. He's in his early thirties, wearing a backpack and carrying a duffel bag.

> GREG
>
> Oh, sorry, sorry. It's this backpack. I don't know where I end.

> BUDDY
>
> Hey, you got the whole *Let's Go Europe* thing happening here. Youth hostels, Eurail pass, yogurt. Get high, see the Anne Frank house.

> GREG
>
> Sorry?

> BUDDY
>
> Join us. Want a drink? Sit down.

> GREG
>
> Thanks, but I just wanted to get something to eat. The line at the snack bar is—

> MIMI
>
> We've got nuts here. Oh, and I got these cheese things.

Mimi's already sized Greg up. Nice enough to share their table, but she'll stick with Buddy for the long haul.

GREG

(looking at the crowd)
Sure, why not? Thanks. Hi.

BUDDY

You got patches on those elbows? Let me guess. English teacher.

Greg takes in Buddy's cell phone, the Rolex, the casual, enormously expensive suit.

GREG

Let *me* guess. Agent.

BUDDY

Advertising.

MIMI

It's like agenting without the heart.

BUDDY

Am I that much of a cliché?

MIMI

Don't look at me. I'm just sitting here eating nuts.

GREG

And I'm not a teacher. I'm a writer.

BUDDY

That's how I started out. Couldn't make a living.

GREG

I write for TV.

BUDDY

Oh, TV? So that "I'm so much better than you" look on your face when I said advertising, I must've imagined that.

MIMI

Maybe on *his* face you imagined it.

GREG

I didn't have any look on my face. Nothing against advertising. It pays me, I guess.

BUDDY

That's right. What do you do?

MIMI

I told you. I work for the National Organ Center. I'm in development.

GUDDY

She's in organ development. You gotta love that.
(he points to a small camera pouch on the table)
You want to see David Crosby? She taped this speech he does about transplants and stuff.

GREG

I write plays, too. That's why I was in Chicago. Play opened.

BUDDY

What TV shows?

MIMI

Good for you. Where?

GREG

It was no big deal. Little theater.

Mimi picks up a newspaper.

MIMI

Really? What's it called? I'm here again next week. I like plays.

GREG

It closed. It was limited run. *Lilacs in the Dooryard.*

BUDDY

I don't even know why they have plays anymore. Hello, we have movies now.

Mimi has found the capsule review section. She flashes a sympathetic look at Greg.

MIMI

Oh. It's not in here.

GREG

Yeah.

BUDDY

What's a dooryard?

GREG

It's from a Whitman poem. "When Lilacs Last in the Dooryard Bloom'd."

BUDDY

(to Mimi)
What the hell's a dooryard?

MIMI

(re: the bar; to Greg)
Oh, they just put sandwiches out. Go on. We'll watch your pack.

He starts to leave, sees a big line at the bar.

> GREG
>
> Maybe I'll just check on my flight. Want me to check yours?

> MIMI
>
> Oh, great. Dallas.

> BUDDY
>
> L.A.

> GREG
>
> Hey, me, too.
> *(to Mimi, pointing to her newspaper so that only she can see it, for not reading the review out loud)*
> Thanks.

He heads off. Mimi watches Buddy closing his eyes, dozing for a second. You can see her deciding to make him luckier . . .

later

Mimi is fooling with her Handycam. She tilts up to FRAME Buddy in her viewfinder. He looks up from the review of Greg's play.

> BUDDY
>
> Jesus. When they don't like something . . .

> MIMI
>
> Oops. Here he comes.
> *(as Greg arrives)*
> We thought we'd lost you.

GREG

You're still scheduled for ten. They say it's gonna take off. Nothing for Dallas yet.

MIMI

It'll be tomorrow at the earliest. The airport hotels must be swamped.

GREG

Oh—take my voucher. It's for the Sheraton. The room's guaranteed. I'm going to stay here, see if something opens up.

BUDDY

You took a bump? When?

GREG

Just now. Hey, two coach tickets anywhere in the U.S — or Mexico —and two hundred dollars. I went to Mexico for this show and I promised the kids I'd take them—

BUDDY

Two hundred? And coach?

GREG

Plus the hotel room. What? I should have haggled?

MIMI

He's pulling your leg. You did great.

GREG

Tell Abby. My wife. I just gave her the good news. I forgot I was supposed to work the Christmas tree lot tomorrow with Scott. Father-son Cub Scout thing, you know.

BUDDY

(Is this guy for real?)
Oh yeah, one of those.

MIMI

Got any pictures?

GREG

Yeah, sure. Here.

He takes out his wallet, shows them to Mimi. Buddy starts playing with the video camera.

MIMI

She's very pretty.

GREG

She and Donna—a neighbor—they had these glamour shots taken at the mall. For a laugh, you know.

BUDDY

(trying to be constructive)
Maybe it's designed for mall lighting.

MIMI

How old are your boys?

GREG

Scott's seven and Joey's four.

BUDDY

Hey look, smile.

MIMI

Jesus, are you recording—

BUDDY

Relax, I fast-forwarded. David Crosby's still here. Smile.

Greg waves at the camera.

GREG

Become a donor. Save a life. Listen to what Crosby said.
(to Mimi)
What did Crosby say?

Mimi grabs the camera from Buddy.

MIMI

"Sorry I drank. Thanks for the liver."

BUDDY

(into camera)
We're here to celebrate the opening and closing of *When Lilacs Something Something Dooryard*, here with the author Greg—

GREG

Janello. Greg Janello.

BUDDY

And all I want to say is the critic for the *Chicago Weekly* is an idiot and an asshole—

GREG

You read the review?

BUDDY

And Abby, whoever you are, forgive him, he did it for you.

OVER THE LOUDSPEAKER, we hear a boarding announcement for Flight 82.

BUDDY

Oops. That's me.

Mimi turns off the camera, puts it in her bag. She glances at Buddy ruefully. Greg notices.

· 12 ·

                             GREG

   Men's room.
   (hand out to Buddy)
   Nice meeting you.

He goes, saluting them both with two fingers to his forehead.

                             GREG

   Later.

He leaves. Mimi looks at Buddy.

                             MIMI

   Well . . .
   (hands him a business card)
   If you ever get to Dallas . . .

Buddy looks at her, smiles.

int. o'hare—infinity gate—waiting area—night

Buddy comes up behind Greg, grabs his arm, and steers him toward the gate. He hands him his boarding pass.

                             BUDDY

   Here. Go sell a Christmas tree for me.

                             GREG

   What?

                             BUDDY

   Go ahead. I want the layover, if you know what I mean.
   Mimi? Organ development? Video camera? Think about it.

Greg doesn't talk about women this way, so he lets the remark slide. Instead he looks at the ticket.

                               GREG
         This is first class—and it's not my name.

                              BUDDY
         They don't check at the gate. And it's a comp.

at the gate

Buddy and Greg have been waiting in this long line, talking. Finally, they're at the head.

                              BUDDY
         I told you, it was free. Enjoy.

                               GREG
         I really appreciate this—

Janice Guerrero joins the other Infinity employee at the gate. Buddy notices her. Damn. He smiles.

                              BUDDY
         Hey.

                              JANICE
         Hello, sir.

Greg hands her his ticket. She feeds it into the machine, hands him the stub.

                               GREG
         Are you sure—

                              BUDDY
         You're doing me a favor. Enjoy.

Greg heads down the gangplank. Janice has her hand out for Buddy's ticket.

JANICE

Your ticket?

BUDDY

You just took it.

JANICE

What?

She looks down, sees Buddy's name on the ticket she collected from Greg.

JANICE

(whispering)
What the hell are you—

BUDDY

(to the other employee)
Would you excuse her for a minute?

He leads her aside.

BUDDY

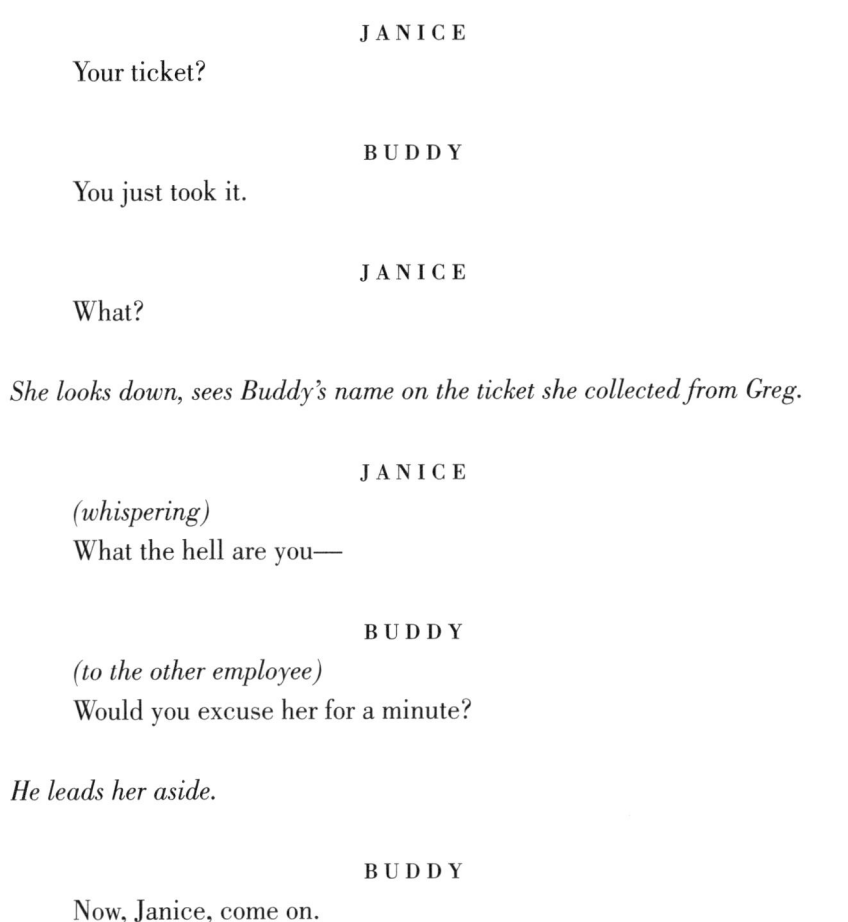

Now, Janice, come on.

long shot (mimi's pov)

Buddy and Janice are talking. Janice isn't happy about something, but she sighs, nods. Buddy turns, heads toward us.

MIMI

Getting into her coat, gathering her bags as Buddy walks up to her. He flashes something in front of her.

BUDDY

His hotel voucher. He insisted.

> (smiling)
> Don't you love air travel?

int. airplane—(in flight)—night

Greg has been drowsing; he casually opens his eyes. It's hushed, quiet, cozy in the first-class cabin. Cabin attendants are chatting; one of them, CAROL WILSON, looks over at him, raises her brows—"Do you want anything?"—he shakes his head no. A couple of passengers—Ron Wachter among them—are watching movies on their private screens. He takes off his headphones, closes his eyes again. A moment.

There's a bump, a bounce. His eyes fly open. Then—

int. o'hare airport sheraton—hotel room—night

A dark room. The clock reads 2:15 A.M. Gradually we become aware of SOUNDS coming from outside and below. Many cars, trucks, and then people calling to one another. Commotion. Suddenly, bright lights go on outside.

The light wakes Buddy. Next to him in bed is Mimi. There are empty cocktail glasses on the nightstand. He staggers up, checks the time, looks out the window to see if it's still snowing.

buddy's pov—outside the hotel

From the second story, Buddy can see lots and lots of camera trucks, taxis, people. A few reporters are already facing cameras, filing reports.

back to scene

Mimi's waking up now.

       MIMI
What time is it?

       BUDDY
Something happened.

He turns on the TV, flips the channels until he finds the news.

tv screen

"FLIGHT 82" is the video banner.

      TV ANNOUNCER
(TV filter)
... here at the O'Hare Airport Sheraton, family and friends of the passengers presumed dead on Flight 82 have gathered to await bulletins from Infinity Airways. Once again, approximately one hour and eight minutes after takeoff, Flight 82 disappeared from radar screens over Kansas ...

Buddy watches, horror-stricken, with Mimi.

int. janello house, chatsworth, ca—master bedroom—night

The PHONE RINGS and ABBY JANELLO, mid-twenties, wakes up and fumbles with it. Abby's hair is trying hard to forget the mall perm it suffered last year; no luck yet. Abby's a good friend, a bad cook, a worse Catholic— a right-to-choose, on-the-pill Catholic, but one who'll still watch any movie with nuns in it. She's the type of feminist who's happy Gloria Steinem got contacts.

                              ABBY

(into phone)
Hello? Mom? What is it, is something wrong? . . .
Chicago. He's coming home tomorrow . . . what? Oh,
Jesus. They said Infinity? . . . No, no, he took another
flight. He called me . . . Mom, stop it—put Les on.
Is Les there? Yeah.

She's fumbling around the covers for the remote, shaken but keeping it together. She finds the notepad by the phone.

                              ABBY

Les? Yeah. What's the number of the flight? . . . Oh thank
God, he's fine, he's coming in on Flight 31, L.A.—it hasn't
even left yet. Tell her . . . what's she saying? . . . Well, maybe
he doesn't know yet. He said they got him a hotel . . . okay,
yeah, I'll call you as soon as I hear. I don't want to tie up the
phone, so . . . right.

She finds the remote, turns on the TV. It doesn't take her long to find the coverage. Her eyes are riveted to the screen. She dials another number without looking at the touchpad.

                              ABBY

(into phone)
Hey, Donna? Yeah, I know. Look, can you come over?

the tv screen

and the coverage of the disaster continues . . .

                         TV ANNOUNCER

. . . would be unlikely to have survived. Witnesses report
seeing a huge fireball seconds after impact . . .

int. hotel room—night

Mimi's on the phone to her husband, her eyes on the TV screen.

                    MIMI

Yes, Roger, I'm fine, I just didn't want you to think I'd been rerouted through L.A. or anything. I'm at the airport . . . I don't have a number—I'll call you as soon as I know what flight I'm on. . . . Well, they're not saying it was weather-related, are they? . . . Okay. Yeah, me, too.

She hangs up as Buddy comes out of the bathroom.

                    MIMI

You gotta call anyone?

                    BUDDY
(holding up a cell phone)
Done. Jesus. Look at me, I'm shaking. That could've been me.

                    MIMI

That poor guy's wife and kids.
(off Buddy's look)
Greg. The guy you switched with.

                    BUDDY

Shit, yeah.
(as he realizes)
They're not going to know he was on there.

int. janello house—kitchen—night

DONNA HEISEN, a believer in everything except pessimism, brings coffee to Abby, who's on the phone. They both whisper to avoid waking the children.

ABBY

Janello, Greg. Is he on that flight? You sure? Yes, that's right, Flight 31, that leaves when? Okay, thank you, thank you.

She hangs up. Donna smiles.

DONNA

See? So you can relax.

ABBY

I just wish he'd call.

DONNA

He's asleep. You don't get news reports when you're asleep.

JOEY

(from the doorway)
Mommy?

They both turn to see JOEY JANELLO, four years old, in the doorway.

ABBY

Hey, big guy, what are you doing up?

JOEY

Can I watch TV?

DONNA

It's the middle of the night, silly. Come on, let Aunt Donna tuck you back in, 'kay?

                             ABBY

I'll take him. Come on, Joey.

CAMERA FOLLOWS ABBY as she walks down the hallway and into:

int. janello house—boys' bedroom—night

SCOTT, seven years old, is asleep. She puts Joey in bed, tucks him in. She looks at them both. Somehow there's a part of her that knows she'll never get back to this moment, when her children are sleeping and their father is coming home to them.

int. o'hare airport—infinity terminal—night

Chaos. Buddy fights his way through the crowds, then sees the woman he's been looking for—Janice Guerrero, the Infinity gate clerk . . .

                            BUDDY

Janice!

She sees him. Her eyes are red.

                            JANICE

Oh my God, Buddy . . . I knew three girls on that crew, and the copilot—

                            BUDDY

We got a problem. The roster's not right.

Janice looks shocked as she remembers.

                            JANICE

Oh, Jesus. Who was he?

BUDDY
You gotta get into the system. Can you do that?

int. janello house—bathroom—day

It's early morning. Abby is wild, red-eyed, washing her face. Donna is trying to cover her own nervousness.

ABBY
What time is it in Chicago?

DONNA
It's nine.

ABBY
Jesus, Donna, where the hell is he?

Scott comes to the bathroom door.

SCOTT
There's somebody at the door.

int./ext. janello house—foyer/front door—day

Abby opens the door. A man and a woman with sad, kind faces stand on the porch.

KEVIN (MAN)
Mrs. Janello?

ABBY
Are you from the airline?

KEVIN
Yes. I'm Kevin Walters and this is Ellen Seitz. Ma'am—

ABBY

He said he was taking a later flight.

ELLEN (WOMAN)

When was the last time you spoke to him?

ABBY

Last night, about eight.

KEVIN

Ten P.M. Chicago.

ELLEN

We have conflicting manifests. One of them—we can't tell yet if it's accurate or not—one of them lists your husband on Flight 82.

ABBY

Well, *I* know. He got bumped. That's what he said.

KEVIN

We have a crisis center at LAX. That's where the first news will be.

ABBY

Just a minute.

She closes the door. From behind her:

DONNA

We'll go together. Jack can watch the boys.

Abby turns to see Donna, whose eyes are full of tears.

ABBY

(her voice tight)
Don't cry, Donna. You're the optimist.

                                    DONNA
    I'm not crying.

But Abby knows better.

int. airplane—(taxiing)—day

Takeoff. Buddy is in first class. Everyone around him is nervous. He's drunk, gripping the armrest of his seat, praying as the plane taxis down the runway.

int. airplane—(in flight)—day

It's quiet. Buddy comes out of the rest room. Sees:

a flight attendant

in the galley, sobbing quietly on the shoulder of an older ATTENDANT. The older Attendant meets Buddy's eyes. He looks away, guiltily . . .

ext. los angeles airport—day

An Infinity 757 touches down.

int. infinity terminal, lax—gate—day

Buddy, pale, baggy-eyed, comes out of the jetway and into the terminal. JIM WELLER, Buddy's partner and quasi-boss, the older brother type, takes his bags, puts a hand on his shoulder. We see him ask, "You okay?" Buddy nods blankly. They make their way through the crowd of reporters and family members.

Up ahead, they see a huge gaggle of reporters. There's a briefing room. He and Jim pass by.

Abby, also blank, sees them. They don't register with her. Kevin and Ellen usher her, with Donna, into another room.

int. counseling room/glass office—day

A commandeered bullpen. Desks, bulletin boards, a desktop Christmas tree in the room beyond this one, a glassed-in office. A fax machine spits out an image that we can't see, but Ellen can, and she picks it up and looks through the window into a larger room, full of family members. She sees Abby and Donna sitting beyond. CAMERA FOLLOWS Ellen as she exits the office into the larger room. Abby doesn't see her until the last moment. She looks up at Ellen, who hands her the paper. Abby looks at it, then drops it to the floor, fumbles for Donna, who grabs her, holds her tight. WE DRIFT DOWN TO SEE A XEROX OF GREG'S LICENSE on the floor.

int. buddy's santa monica condo — day

Before dusk. Buddy and Jim come in. Buddy heads right for the wet bar, makes himself a drink, flips on the TV. It's carrying news reports about the Infinity crash.

Jim joins Buddy in front of the TV. He gently tries to take the bottle away from Buddy.

                              JIM

We got a big day tomorrow. Infinity already called. They want to get in front of this.

                             BUDDY

Yeah.

Jim puts the bottle on the wet bar, prepares to leave. At the door:

> JIM
> Glad you missed that flight, Buddy.

He leaves. Buddy, eyes on the TV, stands up, goes to the wet bar, sits down with the bottle again.

ON TV SCREEN

The newsperson is interviewing THE MAN on page 1 who would've been on the flight but skidded off the road on the way, missed his flight waiting for a tow—and lived.

Match cut to:
living room

Next morning. Buddy wakes up to the angry CAW a phone makes when it's been knocked off the hook. He shakes his head, finds the receiver, puts it on the phone. As soon as he does, the phone rings. He picks it up, listens to an urgent voice, nods. He swallows a mouthful of whiskey, gets going.

ext. buddy's condo — day

A delivered newspaper catches Buddy's eye. On the FRONT PAGE are several stories about Infinity and its fatal crash. Buddy flips through the paper—until he comes upon something that makes him angry . . .

int. tang-weller offices (tang 1) — day

Buddy is storming down a hallway in the offices of Tang-Weller, an advertising firm of 30 employees bursting its seams. He passes several employees; one of them points, mouths "Conference room."

int. tang-weller "war room" (tang 1)—day

Cartons everywhere, menus from takeout places taped on the walls, a conference table that's really just a bunch of desks and tables pushed together. Obviously something is going on: Jim is in a huddle at the far end of the room, and storyboards and mock-ups cover the table. Buddy interrupts a small group by the door. He waves the open newspaper at KAREN, a team leader on the Infinity account, who's standing with LUKE.

> BUDDY
>
> Maybe I'm wrong, but I thought we were trying to create a consistent brand image in the public's eye. The typeface, the logo —who authorized this?

> KAREN
>
> Buddy, come on, it's just telling people who lost relatives what numbers to call, okay? It's not like tomorrow's ad.

> LUKE
>
> Hey, weren't you supposed to be on that flight?

> BUDDY
>
> Like I'd fly in that kind of weather.
> *(to Karen)*
> What do you mean, tomorrow's ad?

Karen gestures to where Jim and another man, TODD EXNER, are talking.

> KAREN
>
> We're getting help. That's Todd Exner. Damage control, spin. Tylenol, ValuJet. Infinity sent him out here this morning to work with us on their condolence ads.

> BUDDY
>
> Condolence ads? Like, sorry we crashed the plane?

                         KAREN
He's been locked up with Josh all morning. But boy, they
sure love my coffee.

Jim is rapping the table for attention.

                          JIM
People, please, we don't have a lot of time today. Todd?

                         EXNER
I'll be brief. I want to thank you all for your ideas. I'm going
to recommend to the board that we go with the concept that
Josh and Sharon have been working on—

                         KAREN
That's Karen, actually.

                         EXNER
It's based on a wire photo out of Chicago . . . I'm going to
need someone to lock up the rights to this pronto —

He and JOSH, a go-getter, unfurl a two-by-three-inch mockup with a laser-printed photo in the center.

poster

Two Infinity employees, in tears, embracing. Behind them, a check-in desk heaped with flowers that people have left there as tributes. Under the photo is a caption: WE GRIEVE FOR OUR PASSENGERS, OUR CREW, AND THEIR FAMILIES.

back to scene

It's pretty moving.

BUDDY

Are you serious? That sentimental, self-serving crap? We're not running that.

EXNER

Excuse me?

BUDDY

No one gives a shit how Infinity feels. Why should they? A plane crashed, fine, there'll be an investigation, it'll be some rudder or hydraulic line or static electricity stuff, whatever. Shit happens, to United, to TWA, to American. Why take responsibility for bad luck?

EXNER

I don't think we want to hide our heads in the sand.

BUDDY

Plus, *you* don't originate campaigns. Neither do you, Josh. We all do. Together. Okay?

JIM

Buddy, nobody's running the ball around you—

EXNER

(directly to Josh)
Okay, let's get on this. I want to fax a copy to the board by noon. *USA Today*, the *New York Times*, the *Chicago Tribune*, and the *L.A. Times*. Come on, let's go!
(he turns to Buddy)
People died here, my friend. Two hundred and sixteen people. You have any idea how much pain that represents? Maybe it's not Infinity's fault, but it happened on their watch. So we shoot this ad and run it tomorrow. And we edit the same kind of thing from news coverage and amateur video and run it on the network news tonight. So I guess my point

is, get your fucking ego out of my way or I'll run it down. *Capisce?*

He leaves. Everyone gets very busy organizing the film shoot, the radio spots, the print ads. Nobody looks at Buddy.

> BUDDY
> How'd I know he was going to wind up saying *capisce?*

Karen flashes him a sympathetic look. Buddy leaves.

int. venice restaurant/bar

A rainy December night. Half-assed Christmas decorations behind the bar. Buddy sees a young woman, FIONA, drinking. Buddy looks like shit but even when he looks like shit, he's better than the slim pickings at this bar. Fiona smiles back.

int. buddy's condo—night

You know the deal here: Buddy rolls off Fiona, unable to stay hard. She looks at him.

> BUDDY
> Sorry, it's not happening.

> FIONA
> Oh, it'll happen. It may not happen the way you like it to happen, but it's gonna happen.

Buddy looks at her, sighs, slides his body down the bed.

later

Buddy's apparently just told her what happened.

FIONA
Oh, God. It coulda been you. It shoulda been you, only you were a nice guy. So it's kind of a sweet story.

BUDDY
Two hundred and sixteen people died.

FIONA
Yeah, on the other hand, definitely. And in a plane, you don't just die. It's dying plus falling. I mean, isn't that like an inborn fear?

BUDDY
You want another drink?

He gets up, goes to the bathroom. The SOUND OF RUNNING WATER.

FIONA
But in a way I kinda think it could be nice. Because other ways, you die alone. In a plane you go with other people. You can hold the person's hand next to you. I mean, you can die in bed and hold someone's hand, but they're not on the same level. They're thinking, Shit, you're a goner and I'm not. Like, what am I gonna have for dinner? So dying in a plane's not pure downside. Hey, that's a joke. Downside. Hello?

No answer from the bathroom. She heads toward it.

int. buddy's bathroom and stall—night

Fiona heads toward the stall, opens the door. Buddy's slumped on the bench in the steam shower, drink in hand. He looks up at her.

>   BUDDY
> What, you want cab fare? Help yourself.

Fiona leaves through the bedroom, furious.

wipe to:
same bed, summer

This time it's Buddy and a second bar girl, SASHA. He's passed out. She sees his wallet. Takes the cash out of it and splits.

wipe to:
same bed, september

Late afternoon. Another girl, obviously a pro, smokes and gets dressed. Buddy looks more than nine months older than the first time we saw him. Plus, he's had a few. He finds something in his wallet as he gets cash to pay her.

>   BUDDY
> Hey. How much if we go out?

>   ZOLA (PRO)
> Huh?

>   BUDDY
> To a function. I have to be at a function.
> *(he shows her the invitation he found)*
> Beverly Hills Hilton.

>   ZOLA
> I need something to wear.

>   BUDDY
> What's wrong with that?

int. beverly hilton ballroom—night

WE'RE SEEING an Infinity Air commercial on a huge projection TV screen. Sentimental music, the kind that makes Pachelbel's Canon sound edgy. This is one of the series of five "We Remember" commercials Tang-Weller did for Infinity during the past nine months. It tells the story of one Infinity flight attendant (CAROL WILSON, page 16) who died in the crash, how her family coped, how they want what she stood for—Infinity Air—to keep burning bright. It sounds like too much, but it's done with enough skill to be effective.

The commercial ends, the lights go up, and we see we're in the ballroom of the Beverly Hilton Hotel.

LOUD APPLAUSE. That was apparently the last clip of the five nominated commercials of the year. Zola, Buddy's pro date, is SOBBING LOUDLY. Buddy, really drunk now, is rolling his eyes. Jim, Karen, Josh, and Todd Exner are also at the table; no one seems delighted that Buddy could make it.

                         BUDDY

Makes you wish you crashed more often, doesn't it, Todd? Makes Infinity so damn human.

                         ZOLA

(sincerely, tearful)
They always find a burned doll. That's what gets me. And it's funny, you never see any dolls on planes that don't crash.

                         EMCEE

(at the podium)
And this year's winner for Best National Campaign is Tang-Weller, client Infinity Air, "We Remember" series.

At the table, Jim gets up.

BUDDY

Hey, that's my account.

JIM

Buddy, please—

EXNER

Can't you control this idiot?

Jim tries to reason with Buddy, but Buddy stumbles on up to the podium, takes the award from the presenter. He stands there a moment, sweating, drunk, squinting at the crowd.

BUDDY

Thank you, thank you for this award. Gee, it's so heavy, aren't I supposed to say that? Or, "Oh, so this is what these look like up close." It's good to see you all. I haven't been around much this year. See, I was supposed to be on that flight. Isn't that ironic? I coulda been one of those people up there who believed so much in Infinity Air I was glad to die, just so's it could get all this great attention on how well it handled it. Isn't that what we're saying? Hey, we crashed, but man, we're hurting and we're humble, and we're ready to sell tickets, right?

Jim is now at the podium. Into the microphone:

JIM

Thank you, ladies and gentlemen. Thank you.

He tries to lead Buddy off the stage.

BUDDY

Shame about the dead people, but hey, it's an ill wind, right? Blew us right onto the map!

He stumbles, Jim straightens him up, and then Buddy passes out, hits the floor with a sickening thud.

back at the table

They're all stunned, humiliated. Except Zola.

                    ZOLA

Is there a party after?

fade out:

fade in:
ext. desert drug & alcohol center, rancho mirage—day

TITLE: ninety DAYS LATER. Jim is walking Buddy to the car, carrying Buddy's suitcase. Buddy carries a canvas tote bag.

                    JIM

You should take your time easing back in. We're in good shape.

                    BUDDY

How can you be in good shape? I've been away for three months.

                    JIM

You've been away for a year, but who's counting. You look good. Think it'll take? I mean, you feel good?

Buddy nods, looks up at the sky. A plane flies overhead. Buddy's expression changes slightly, but he forces a smile.

int. tang-weller (tang 1)—night

The banners slung from the rafters tell us it's a welcome back party for Buddy Amaral. Buddy's in mid-speech.

BUDDY

I'm sorry I had to put you guys through this whole Twelve-step trip, it's so eighties, but you know . . . I feel better, I feel great. And I hear you guys've been busy while I was gone—Southern California Toyota dealers, that's great, Josh—and we got a lot of great things ahead—bigger offices, for one, so Jim tells me—and so, even though New Year's is a couple days away—here's to the future. Is this apple juice?
(Jim tastes it, nods)
I got my own taster now. Like Nero.
(he holds up his drink)
To the future.

buddy's office

Later. Jim is showing Buddy a manila folder filled with photos of an office building.

JIM

Two floors, twenty-four thousand square feet, employee and client parking, and within one block two banks, a Kinko's, and a couple dozen Starbucks.

BUDDY

What's the rent?

JIM

Oh no, we buy. Already got a deal with the owner—he wants out of the landlord business. Old guy, not too savvy, he'll do it at one-eight— *and* without a broker.

                    BUDDY

When can I see it? Assuming you want my input?

                    JIM

Anytime you want—the tenants are already out. It's great, Buddy. You're gonna love it. Don't fight it because you were out of the loop. We didn't want to bother you.

                    BUDDY

Hey, Jim, come on. It'll be great. Really. Excuse me.

int. tang-weller men's room (tang 1)—night

Later. Buddy's washing his hands, looking at himself in the mirror. We can HEAR the sounds of the party through the door. His apple juice is on the ledge in front of him. Further down is another glass, abandoned, half-full of what looks like scotch. Buddy looks at it, sidles down to it, lifts it to his nose. From behind him:

                    SETH (O.S.)

You sure you wanna do that?

Buddy turns to see SETH, twenty-five, Starbucks-ish, not particularly ingratiating, standing at the urinal. He nods toward the glass.

                    BUDDY

Oh. Jesus—thought it was my glass. See, here's mine. Apple juice.

                    SETH

Right.

Buddy watches him in the mirror as he finishes washing his hands.

SETH

(without turning around)
You don't want to stare at me like that, not in the men's room. It's sexual harassment.

BUDDY

Are you kidding me? I'm not gay.

SETH

Yeah, but I am.
(he zips up, comes to the sink)
And you're my boss, at least officially, so . . .

BUDDY

Since when?

SETH

Since a week after they shipped you to Palm Springs. You had some breakdown during an awards ceremony? That's what I heard.

BUDDY

It wasn't a breakdown. It was an episode. So what do you do here?

SETH

P.A. Office floater. Handle the computers, mostly. You guys have some real Jurassic hardware here.
(indicates the glass)
Would that've been your first drink since they released you?

BUDDY

You got a lot of nerve, kid.

SETH

Relax, I'm a drunk, too. Six years sober. AA and NA.

BUDDY

And we hired you?

SETH

I had to sign a "no-episode" clause, but yeah. Look, you want some help with your reentry, I'm happy to oblige. Just don't screw up. Lot of nice people working here. Why should they pay for your shit?

BUDDY

Because I own twenty percent of the company? And in case you were picking pimples when they covered this at your rehab, alcoholism's a disease.

SETH

Yeah, you catch it from open bottles.

BUDDY

You're not going to make me feel guilty over something I had no control of.

SETH

Oh, so you're that type. When was the last time something was your fault?

BUDDY

I can't believe this guy.

SETH

They do AA where they dried you out? You know, the Twelve Steps, all that jazz?

BUDDY

They tried. I don't believe in God.

SETH

Man, he'll be crushed when he finds out. You're not going to last a week sober.

                              BUDDY
        Fuck you.

                              SETH
        Welcome back, boss.

He leaves.

                              BUDDY
        P.S., you're fired.

But the door has closed and nobody's heard him. He slams the plastic glass onto the floor.

int. buddy's condo—bedroom—night

Buddy's in bed, lights out but awake.

int. buddy's condo—kitchen/living room—night

Buddy opens the refrigerator. Shelf upon shelf of diet drinks, apple juice, and Perrier. He goes to the living room. The tote he brought out of the treatment center is on the dining table. He dumps it out on the table. There's a copy of the AA textbook, Alcoholics Anonymous. *He flips through it.*

buddy's pov—the twelve steps

He looks at Step 8: "Made a list of all persons we had harmed and became willing to make amends to them all."

back to buddy

Something about this grabs him. He thinks—then he searches—his bookcase, a basket full of magazines, his desk. Finally, he finds it in a closet:

people magazine

The cover story: "Flight 82. The Last Trip for 216 Very Ordinary, Very Special People."

back to scene

Buddy flips through it till he finds Greg's picture. We hear the SCREECH of a MODEM HANDSHAKE . . .

computer screen

A Web site, a phone/address database. Typing appears on the screen: JANELLO, GREG. Buddy types in area codes: 213, 323, 818, 310. Finally, an address appears: 14398 Jewell Ave., Chatsworth.

Buddy stares at it.

ext. jewell avenue, chatsworth—day

Morning. Buddy is in his car, watching the door. He's about to get out when the door opens and Abby comes out, wrestling with a large Rottweiler. In the year since her husband's death, she's gotten a haircut. We hope she didn't pay much for it. The house looked better a year ago; the lawn is brown.

She wrestles the dog into her car and pulls out.

Buddy follows in his car.

ext. strip mall—sherman way—day

Abby pulls into this strip mall, which is maybe two years old. Buddy parks across the street.

The mall has only one shop open for business, a dry cleaner with Spanish window signs. The rest of the building is vacant, two stories of mostly white-soaped windows.

Abby uses her key to enter one of the ground-floor storefronts. It has a sign on the door that reads VINEGROVE REALTY, *but above the door is a sign reading* COPIES. *Half these windows are soaped, half-mini-blinded.*

A moment later Abby lugs a sign out to the parkway, one of those signs that rotates in the wind. One side reads TODAY; *the other,* LEASING. *She goes back in the shop.*

on buddy

In his car. The widow's alive; she survived; she has a job. She even has a dog. He could turn back now . . .

the storefront door

Later. Buddy tries to peek in. He breathes, decides, opens the door. It's locked.

> ABBY (O.S.)
> Just a minute!
> *(to the dog; urgent whisper)*
> Come on, boy! Back. Okay, okay, in here. There's your toy!

There are some STRANGE NOISES and then, finally, Abby opens the door. She's harried; a little wary. Her whole attitude says, "Don't surprise me." Her smile is tense.

                    ABBY
Hi. Hello. I'm sorry. I had to lock the dog in the bathroom. All of the storefronts have bathrooms, of course, which are large enough for storage. Hi. Abby Janello, Vinegrove Realty.

Buddy smiles, puts out his hand to meet hers.

                    BUDDY
Buddy Amaral. Hi. I was just driving by and saw your sign—

                    ABBY
Look, the dog's not supposed to be here, but my friend who was going to watch him—he can't be left alone—she has a doctor's appointment. Everything's fine and then, you know. Involuntary urination.

                    BUDDY
Hope the doctor doesn't keep her waiting.

                    ABBY
No, the dog. Oh, you're kidding. Funny. This is a wonderful property. Are you interested? We got two units with a thousand square feet, and one upstairs with two but we can subdivide, that's not a problem. You want to check it out?

int. storefront—day

Not much here: the old counter from the copy shop, a phone, a couple chairs. The dog is throwing itself against the bathroom door. Abby doesn't acknowledge it, though the effort costs her. She gives him her spiel as she waves her hand in front of her, trying to dispel cigarette smoke. She picks up a Diet Coke can which is smoking; she rattles it to soak the butt inside.

ABBY

(lying)
I'm sorry, the last person I showed this to smoked. There's been a lot of interest in these units. Here's a setup and my card; I'm in between beeper numbers so ignore that. The building's two years old, very well built, with entirely new management. The comps in the area—we're about fifty cents a square foot less, and if you take one of the first two units, there's an additional discount—what business are you in?

Throughout this the BARKING has been DEAFENING.

BUDDY

Maybe if you let him out?

ABBY

Would you be interested in a ground floor unit? There *is* an elevator if you'd rather be up.

BUDDY

What's his name?

ABBY

(hesitating)
Fred.

BUDDY

Fred?

ABBY

He doesn't like people and he's not trained, I've only had him a year—

                    BUDDY

It's okay, Fred. Good boy, good boy.

The dog stops BARKING.

                    BUDDY

See? I've got a way with dogs. And Rotties are great. I had one when I was a kid.

This is a mistake. How'd he know it was a Rottweiler? Abby is instantly on edge.

                    ABBY

Yes, they are. You know what, maybe we should do this another time. I'm expecting my boss any minute. Why don't you come back around noon?

                    BUDDY

Excuse me?

                    ABBY

I didn't say it was a Rottweiler. Okay?

                    BUDDY

I . . . I saw you go into the building, that's all.

                    ABBY

That was half an hour ago. You said you were passing by—

                    BUDDY

I did, I saw you on my way to a meeting, and on my way back I—

Abby has managed to get over to the bathroom door. The dog is BARKING AGAIN.

ABBY

I mean it! If you say one more word, I'm going to open this door!

BUDDY

You don't understand—

Abby opens the door and the dog bounds out, barking furiously at Buddy, its hair on edge.

BUDDY

All right, all right, fine. I'm sorry. I just—

ABBY

Get out!

The dog takes this as a command. He rushes for Buddy, jumps on him. Buddy tumbles to the ground.

Abby is SCREAMING, Buddy is YELLING, trying to keep the dog away from his throat with his hands. The dog rips his jacket sleeve off.

ABBY

Buddy! Buddy! Stop it!

BUDDY

Hey, lady, I'm just lying here—

ABBY

Not you, the dog. Buddy! Buddy!

She pulls the dog off Buddy, manages to wrestle him back into the bathroom.

BUDDY

You said his name was Fred! I probably pissed him off, calling him Fred!

ABBY
(still irritated)
What was I supposed to do? You can't go around telling clients they've got a dog's name! Are you all right?

She is fumbling for cigarettes, lights one.

BUDDY
The jacket, the pants . . . Jesus. I didn't see a license, does it have a license?

ABBY
Look, I can't lose this job. If you make trouble, I . . . Please. You gotta let me take care of it.

ext. back of the strip mall—day

Two open doors— one to the store Abby was showing Buddy, one to the dry cleaners. Abby and Buddy sit on the curb. She's stuffing a freshly lit cigarette into the Coke can/ashtray. They are watching Buddy the dog sniff around the Dumpster.

ABBY
I got him for the kids last year. They like him, it's just. . . . He's a lot of work. And I think they kinda look at him as this booby prize for their father . . .
(off Buddy's look)
Oh. He d— He divorced me last year. We divorced each other.

BUDDY
Oh.

ABBY
I wasn't trying to buy them off, I swear. Maybe I thought it'd be a distraction. It worked better with Joey. He's five.

                    BUDDY
I was almost married once. Couple years ago.

                    ABBY
What happened?

                    BUDDY
Oh, you know. I don't know. Some couples are lucky and some aren't.

                    ABBY
Yeah, I know. We weren't too lucky. He was a TV writer—did you ever see *Midnighter*? It was syndicated. He did some episodes. I mean, he's still doing them, he's on staff now.

She has put a cigarette in her mouth. Buddy lights it.

                    BUDDY
You only took two puffs out of the last one.

                    ABBY
I don't really smoke. Last year I started chewing the gum, Donna was giving up smoking, and it sort of helps the nerves, and then I got hooked on the gum, and then I got TMJ, you know, from chewing, so this is just to help me quit the gum. I'm ten days off the gum.

                    BUDDY
Sounds like a good plan. By next week you'll be on heroin.

A WOMAN steps outside from the dry cleaners behind them, shouts "Ready!" to Buddy.

                    ABBY
See. One hour or less. And here . . .

She takes out a deposit slip from her checkbook and rips off her address and hands it to him.

                    ABBY
. . . When you get them rewoven, send the bill to me, okay?

                    BUDDY
It's fine—all right.

They both stand up. We see that Buddy's wearing a pair of bright sweatpants he borrowed from the dry cleaners.

                    BUDDY
Well. It was nice meeting you and Buddy.

                    ABBY
I was right. You didn't really want to see any space, did you?

                    BUDDY
(holding up the manila envelope)
Copies. The sign's still up. And then you launched into your spiel, and then the dog, and—

                    ABBY
(mortified)
Oh, yeah, right. Well. Sorry again.

He walks next door to the dry cleaners, goes inside. Abby watches him, then looks off at Buddy the dog.

                    ABBY
(hand to her nose)
Oh, for God's sake . . . what the hell did you eat this morning?

She grabs a piece of newspaper, heads toward him . . .

int. dry cleaners—day

Buddy's behind a screen, changing into his mended suit. He hears Abby calling, "Buddy! Buddy!" He sees her wrestling the dog back into the building.

int. tang-weller (tang 1)—buddy's office—night

Empty office, except for Buddy. He's reviewing ANIMATIC VIDEOS on the TV, dictating his notes. He notices a folder on the coffee table; opens it: it contains the pictures of the building Jim found.

ext. janello house—night

ABBY (O.S.)
Joey! Five more minutes and I'm gonna come in and wash your hair!

int. janello house—kitchen—night

Abby is cooking dinner while Donna helps her fold laundry.

DONNA
Did you see a ring?

Abby flashes her a look as Scott comes in, opens the oven door.

SCOTT
You're not gonna get in. He locked the door. He said the bubbles are gone and you can see it.

ABBY
Honey, go in there and wash his hair, okay? Go on, go!

He leaves, goes down the hall. Abby waits a beat.

> ABBY
>
> No, I didn't see a ring. And I didn't not see a ring. I didn't look.

> DONNA
>
> Yeah, right. Was he cute?

> ABBY
>
> I don't know. Kind of. Not suburban. Not a soap-on-a-rope, Sears-Best kind of guy.

> DONNA
>
> I like soap-on-a-rope guys.

> ABBY
>
> I just hope his pants don't cost me an arm and a leg. They're lined.

Donna looks impressed. The phone rings. Abby snaps it up.

> ABBY
>
> *(into phone)*
> Hello? This is her, she. Oh. Yes, of course. Um, did you get an estimate on the pants?

Donna is all ears.

intercut with:
int. buddy's office—night

He's on the phone, flipping through the real estate folder Jim gave him.

BUDDY

(into phone)
No, no, forget about the suit. It's business. You've got a realtor's license, right?

ABBY

Of course—

BUDDY

See, the thing is, my firm, Tang-Weller, we're relocating, and our current realtors aren't cutting it and I thought, you know, maybe you could help.

ABBY

Me? But I—

BUDDY

We've got seven thousand square feet in Culver City and we need like, three, four times as much. To buy, not lease. You think you can help? Somewhere under two?

ABBY

Million? Two million?

BUDDY

Yeah. What do you think?

Abby's doing the commission math on a pad of paper. Her share, three percent, would come to $60,000.

ABBY

But . . . why me? I don't have the experience.

BUDDY

You'll work harder. You're hungry.

ABBY

I'm hungry because I suck, okay? Look, let me have you call Norma, she handles all of this stuff.

BUDDY

I'd like you to. Can you come in Monday at ten? It'd be great if you had one or two properties to show us right then. Somewhere in the same area—Marina del Rey, Venice, Culver City . . .

ABBY

Wait a minute, hold on here—

BUDDY

There's only one thing. There's a property I want you to show us on Abbott Kinney. Have you got a pen? 18385 Abbott Kinney Boulevard. That's Venice. The guy's ready to sell, doesn't have a broker, so maybe you could book a double commission, you know? Can you set it up for us to see at eleven?

ABBY

I can talk to him, sure, but—

BUDDY

Great. I'll call you at your office tomorrow and fax over the specifics, what we're looking for, that kind of thing. You okay with this?

ABBY

Yeah, sure, fine. Thanks. Okay. I guess.

BUDDY

Great. Good night.

She hangs up.

                    ABBY

He wants to give me some business.

                    DONNA

I'll bet.

                    ABBY

I'm calling him back.

                    DONNA

Hey, he's interested, Abby. You're interested. It's okay. It's been a year. It's time.

                    ABBY

Yeah, time to make some money, Donna, that's all. God. Down, girl.

But she's intrigued—pleased. Donna watches her, smiles.

int. tang-weller (tang 1)—buddy's office—day

Monday morning. Buddy, carrying a large glass-framed poster, bounces into his office only to discover Seth there.

                    BUDDY

Where's Judy?

                    SETH

Wichita. Her sister had an aneurysm last night. Dropped dead. Three kids.
(handing him his messages)
She's there twice. Number two says she's quitting. Want me to get her for you?

                    BUDDY

Call her, tell her I'm sorry, send some flowers. I'll get her later.

(reading a message)
Yeah, tell Josh I got his third-quarter media plan and it bites.

SETH

And Jim's been buzzing about this ten o'clock you put on his calendar.

BUDDY

I'll handle it. And hide this. And the others in reception. *(pointing to Judy's "Hang On—Friday's Coming" poster)*
And you can get rid of that now, too, while you're at it.

Buddy's off. Seth looks at the poster, which shows one of their campaigns for Infinity Air.

int. tang-weller (tang 1)—jim's office— day

JIM

But I don't want a broker. This deal doesn't need a broker.

BUDDY

I know, I know. Look, it's just a couple hours.

JIM

I found the place! We're not going to find anything better!

BUDDY

You know that, I know that, so big deal. Look, she's starting over, you know. She's had a tough year.

JIM

Oh, she in one of your groups? 'Cause I haven't heard you mention them.

                            BUDDY
Anyway, we let her take us around to two, three properties,
I've done my bit.
(as Jim hesitates)
I know you want to be supportive.

                             JIM
(not too annoyed)
You can play that card once, pal, and you just used it up. Fine.

int. tang-weller lobby (tang 1)— day

Abby enters, looks around nervously. She's taken some time with her appearance. She goes to the receptionist.

                            ABBY
Hi. I'm Abby Janello. I'm here to see Buddy Amaral. I'm early. Should I sit down? Oh, sorry.

The receptionist, headsetted, is obviously trying to listen to a conversation in her ear. Abby looks at the framed ad campaign posters on the walls. There are three blank spaces where Infinity Air ads used to be. From behind her:

                            BUDDY
Abby? Hey.

                            ABBY
Oh. Hi. I hope you're not getting too optimistic.
(off his look, she indicates the empty walls)
You're packing already?

                            BUDDY
Oh, there was something wrong with the matte jobs. I don't think they were acid-free, which is key for matting.

(a little awkwardness)
You should always make sure your mattes are acid-free, otherwise they'll, uh . . .

ABBY

Have acid?

BUDDY

Exactly.

An awkward pause. Abby doesn't know they're waiting for Jim.

ABBY

I read the material you faxed me. About your business and your setup here. I don't know much about advertising. If you don't count *Bewitched*.

BUDDY

Well, we got our share of twitching noses but with our drug-intervention program, that's on the decline. Joke.

ABBY

(sincerely)
Yes, very funny.

BUDDY

Did you find any properties?

ABBY

Yeah, I, uh, I have three, besides the one you mentioned.

BUDDY

The owner gave you the listing?

ABBY

Yeah, but I had to promise him I'd get him a higher price to make up for the commission. He's got a half-assed offer for one-eight but it smells fishy—

BUDDY

Yeah, look—when you bring it up to Jim, pretend you found it.

ABBY

Who's Jim?

BUDDY

My partner. Partner-boss, sort of. Larry Tate, remember him? He doesn't always like my ideas, so if you say it was yours . . .

ABBY

Oh, look, I don't know—

Suddenly Jim enters the lobby, a good-sport smile on his face.

JIM

Ah, you must be—

ABBY

Abby Janello, Vinegrove Realty. Hi. You must be Larry.

BUDDY

Jim.

ABBY

Jim. Pleased to meet you.

JIM

Hey, a friend of Buddy's. . . . You two meet out in Palm Springs?

ABBY

No, no. I—

BUDDY

Well, we better get rolling. You parked on the street?

JIM

I've got the attorney meeting at 1:00, so let's take two cars . . .

BUDDY

(to Abby)
I'll drive us. That okay with you?

ABBY

Sure, okay. Great. I just left some papers in my car, so . . .

BUDDY

We'll meet you out front.

She gathers her things, smiles, leaves. Buddy thumps Jim on the sleeve.

BUDDY

Don't mention Palm Springs. It's anonymous, remember?

JIM

Did you make another Larry Tate crack before I came in?

int. buddy's car—culver city—(moving)—day

Buddy's driving; Abby's riding shotgun. She's nervous, rifling through her papers.

ABBY

Wow, he's picky. I thought he'd like that one.

BUDDY

Yeah, I think we're about to lose him. Let me see what else you've got.
(flipping through her folder)
Tell you what. Let's go with this one on Abbott Kinney, and I'll look at the rest with you.
(he pauses as Abby doesn't react)
What?

ABBY

Oh, it's nothing. It's just your compass. You don't see a lot of them anymore.

Buddy looks at the compass he has mounted on his dash.

BUDDY

Superstitious. Had one in my first car, never had an accident.

ABBY

Lucky you. Okay. So turn here.

int. jim's car— (moving)— day

Jim's driving, following Buddy's car. He's on his cellular phone; he stops talking as he sees where Buddy's pulled in.

JIM

Shit.

They've stopped in front of Jim's find: the building in the Polaroids.

ext. abbott kinney blvd., venice— day

Jim parks his car, bounds out to take Buddy's arm.

JIM

(his eyes on the building)
Buddy? Could I speak to you?

ABBY

It's okay, I have others . . .

JIM

(undertone)
This is the building.

BUDDY

Oh, you think so? Good.

JIM

No, this is the building. I mean, the one I want. The photos?

BUDDY

Oh. Wow. Well, I gave her the specs we were looking for— I guess there's only so much inventory on the market.

JIM

I'm gonna kill him, we had a deal and he went to a broker. We can't let her show it to us, we got to leave before his broker shows up —you see him?

BUDDY

(to Abby)
What time is the seller's broker due here?

ABBY

I'm the seller's broker. It's my listing. Exclusive. So I've got the keys right here.

She unlocks the door, breezes in . . .

                    BUDDY
What are you gonna do? Fate.

int. empty office building (empty tang 2)—day

Abby is leading Jim through the building. She's selling the hell out of it, trying not to worry about Jim's sour look. Buddy watches her. He catches her eye; she smiles uncertainly. He smiles back.

ext. office building (tang 2)—day

Jim comes out onto the street, followed by Buddy. Abby locks up, gathers her strength, approaches them.

                    ABBY
I'm sorry about this one—it was just a wild guess—I have two others for today and I can get some more together for later in the week—

                    JIM
Let's go back to the office and talk an offer. Goddammit.

He goes off to his car. Abby looks at Buddy, astonished and puzzled. He shrugs his shoulders.

int. buddy's office—day

Jim, Abby, and Buddy are in Buddy's office. Seth comes in and out with coffee, files, etc.

ABBY

Listen, I understand your disappointment, but you really didn't have a deal. The seller was bound to get some advice and believe me, no one'd let him do a deal this size without a broker or lawyer or someone.

JIM

So how'd he happen to find you?

ABBY

I approached *him*. Look, he's going to list at two-one. That's still under market.

JIM

He was gonna sell it to me for one-point-eight.

Abby takes out a kind of slide-rule mortgage calculator.

ABBY

Say you go in at one-nine. What are you putting down?

JIM

We were thinking thirty percent— of one-eight. And a fixed at eight and a half.

ABBY

You'd be tying up a lot of cash for a commercial property. I'd go in at twenty, twenty-five at the most, free up some of that money. Thirty percent at one-point-eight is what, 540K? I say we go in at twenty percent of one-nine, that's 380K, meaning we finance one-five-twenty at seven and three quarter percent—and I can source that cheaper for you—that's ten-eight-eighty a month. That's a difference of twelve hundred a month. You can pass that on easy.

Buddy watches her. She knows her stuff.

                         JIM
I don't know.

                         ABBY
You waiting for me to offer to kick in some commission?

                         JIM
Well . . . it's an easy deal. It's not like you had to knock yourself out for six months finding it.

                         ABBY
Okay. One point. That's a check for 20K at close of escrow. But that's it. Because he can get two-point-one if he wants to wait even two months. But hey, whatever you want.

She starts to stand up —but Jim stops her.

                         JIM
All right. One-nine. Bring it by my office and I'll sign.

                         ABBY
Oh. Well, thank you. Yes, I will.

Jim leaves. The door closes.

                         BUDDY
Wow. How long you been doing this?

                         ABBY
Oh my God, I don't know where the words came from. I feel terrible about lying, though.

                         BUDDY
You didn't lie, you just didn't tell the whole truth.

ABBY

Like I tell my kids, that's called lying. God, Norma's going to die. I mean, this is so out of my league. I always got the feeling she gave me the job out of pity.
(she catches herself)
My divorce and all.

BUDDY

Maybe this'll get you off strip mall patrol.

ABBY

Wouldn't that be great.
(casually)
Why'd he think we met in Palm Springs? Is he getting me mixed up with some girlfriend?

BUDDY

I don't know. I might have mentioned you were a friend of a friend. Jim doesn't like realtors. I'm the salesman, I like salesmen. He doesn't.

ABBY

Greg had a thing against salesmen, too. He wouldn't let Scott sell chocolate bars for the school. Didn't want his kid selling anything. I mean, still doesn't. And now *I* am. Funny. Okay, can I write this up here? And thanks. I owe you.

Buddy waves her gratitude away . . .

int. abby's house—bedroom/kitchen—night

Abby's awake, 3:00 A.M. She pads down the hallway. Opens the door of the boys' room: Scott and Joey are both asleep. In the kitchen she puts some Swiss Miss and three packs of Equal in a mug, runs hot water onto it.

flashback—abby and greg

A quick hug and kiss from Greg one late night in the kitchen.

back to abby

Blank. No tears. She just breathes.

int. abby's house—garage—night

The light comes on and Abby comes out. She gets into Greg's car, a big, boxy Buick convertible with a bench front seat. Obviously she spends a lot of time here. There are magazines, a box of cookies in the glove compartment. It smells like him. She turns on the overhead light, switches on the radio and starts reading a magazine. We notice a compass, just like the one in Buddy's car, mounted on the dash . . .

ext. abby's backyard—day

It's a March day, and Abby and her neighbor Donna are cleaning out Abby's gutters.

> ABBY
> And on Friday, the deal closes and they give me a desk—with a computer and my own partition. You know. Instead of working at the floater's desk.

> DONNA
> Everything's about perception, you know? Suddenly you're perceived differently.

> ABBY
> Yeah, I'm perceived as the girl with her own partition.

DONNA

Oops, watch it. Dead bird.

ABBY

You've got gloves on.

DONNA

Your gutters, not mine.

Abby fishes it out, grimaces.

ABBY

It's kind of amazing you don't see more dead birds. Considering there's billions of them. Considering how often you see bird shit.

DONNA

Obviously they're going to go to the bathroom more than they die. Everyone does.

ABBY

Go to the bathroom? Honey, they don't go to the bathroom, okay? They shit.

DONNA

Do they pee or is it all one thing? Kelly asked me that the other day.

Donna is raking the crap that Abby throws down into piles.

ABBY

What I don't get is why this guy did it.

DONNA

Haven't we been through this?

ABBY
I know what we thought, but he hasn't called me since, you know, with made-up reasons. We had a forty-five-day escrow, I heard from him maybe twice—with legitimate questions. I've talked to his partner or boss or whatever more. Not that I care. It's too soon.

DONNA
It's never gotten personal?

ABBY
I know he's single. He knows I am.

DONNA
That's probably why he hasn't called. My mother said after she was a widow people were like scared of her or something.

ABBY
I told him I was divorced. Norma said don't mention death in a negotiation.

DONNA
Norma. Anyway, you're probably right. He's shy or scared and you're not interested, so forget about it. I mean, it's not like you can ask him for a date . . .

int. tang-weller (tang 1)—kitchen—day

Buddy's looking at some storyboards with Luke; Seth's in the b.g. fixing his lunch.

BUDDY
You're gonna have trouble with legal on eight. Forget it, let them tell us. Ship it.

Luke nods, leaves—and Buddy sees Abby coming his way.

BUDDY

Hey! What are you doing here?

ABBY

Well, um, I guess, in the area. Looks like the move is on track.

BUDDY

This weekend. Phone guys are over there now.

ABBY

And, uh—I wanted to, uh . . .

BUDDY

What?

ABBY

I wanted to thank you, so I . . .
(she pulls out a small tickets envelope)
I got tickets for the Dodgers. I know you like them, I saw your coffee mug. They're for Friday. I thought we could . . . you know. Go. If you want. Or you could just have them. Both, if you're seeing . . . if you have a friend who likes them. I'm fine either way.

Buddy's trapped. He doesn't want to encourage her; doesn't want to hurt her either.

BUDDY

Oh. Well, thank you. But . . .
(sudden relief)
Oh shit, Friday? That's too bad. We got a business dinner, these clients in from San Francisco. Otherwise. Sorry—

Seth heads out of the kitchen with his lunch.

SETH

No, that's been moved to Monday. Remember? And it's lunch.

He breezes on into the office. Buddy shoots him a dirty look, then turns back to Abby, smiling.

BUDDY

That's great. Great. Dodgers, huh?

int. dodger stadium— day

Buddy looks down at the rows of seats, sees Abby. Does he really want to go through with this? Then he sees Abby preventing a man from sitting in the seat next to her, anxiously looking around for Buddy.

Buddy's not heartless. He goes down the steps to her row, calls out to her. Her face lights up.

int./ext. dodger stadium—night

The Dodger game. Abby and Buddy watch, cheer. Buddy turns to look at her once, watches her total absorption in the game.

int. dodger stadium— concession area—night

Buddy comes out of the men's room, sees Abby in a long line for the women's room. So he keeps her company, chatting as the line moves slowly. . . . The other women in the line envy her for his gallantry. She notices their envy; agrees.

int. pann's coffee shop—night

Buddy and Abby are studying the menu. They've got a seat next to the rest rooms. A teenage girl comes out, trailing toilet paper from her shoe, heading back to her big date. Abby's out of her chair like a shot, menu in hand, runs behind the girl, steps on the toilet paper. The girl moves on unencumbered. Abby returns to her seat, struggling herself with the toilet paper on her heel now, and opens her menu as if nothing happened. Buddy watches her. Some woman.

ext. pann's coffee shop—parking lot—night

Buddy and Abby have closed down the coffee shop. As they leave, the lights go out. They walk to Abby's car. Buddy opens the door for her. They are both strangely reluctant to end the evening.

ABBY

You want to sit for a while?

Buddy knows what's waiting for him at home. Nothing.

BUDDY

Yeah, sure.

She gets in, leans across the bench front seat, flips up the passenger door lock. Buddy gets in.

int. abby's car—(stationary)—night

Buddy settles in, studies the car.

BUDDY

This isn't yours, is it?

ABBY

It's Greg's. My . . . ex. Mine's in the shop, so . . .

Buddy notices the compass. He gives it a twirl.

ABBY

Sitting in cars at the diner. I never did that, did you?

BUDDY

No, not really. No diners. Bars.

ABBY

How much of our life do we spend looking at dashboards, when you think about it? Dashboards and TV. And acoustic ceilings.

BUDDY

Too much.

ABBY

I had a baby in a car. Joey. Well, not exactly in the car, we made it to the ER. Not this car, it was a Gremlin, remember those? I had it in school. And I was . . . Greg was driving and I just knew I was gonna have this baby, and he wouldn't pull over, and I got this idea in my head that I didn't want to have the baby in the front seat, that it wouldn't be safe, so I tried to climb into the back, and I broke Greg's nose with my foot. I had a contraction and pow, I got him right there. And he couldn't drive, I mean, the blood was pouring, so I had to the rest of the way, screaming and crying and driving. God. And he had a beautiful nose. A good face, you know, handsome, but a beautiful nose. That's all I could think of the whole time I was delivering: I ruined his nose. And later—he didn't know he did this—whenever we'd have a fight, he'd touch his nose, like Danny Kaye in *White Christmas* with the arm. Like, "You owe me, pal." It used to make me so angry.

She's smiling—and then looks at Buddy, who's staring at her like she's some kind of miracle.

ABBY

What?

BUDDY

I just . . . I don't know how women get so brave. That's all.

ABBY

You think that's brave? I was so scared. I'm always scared.

BUDDY

It's not brave if you're not scared.

Abby takes this in, touched. It's maybe the nicest thing anyone's ever said to her.

ABBY

Well. You have a good face, too.

She touches his face. Suddenly, it's impossible to tell who moves first, who is kissing whom. But they kiss, a long, lingering kiss that surprises them both. It's just as hard to tell who pulls back first.

ABBY

Thank you. Well, okay. Good night.

Buddy looks stunned—and like he wants to take it all back.

BUDDY

Okay, well. Thanks for the tickets. Good night.

He gets out, walks to his car, worried.

int. buddy's condo—night

Buddy comes in. He's shaken. He goes to the refrigerator, looks for something to drink. Searches the kitchen for some booze, looks in the wet bar. Nothing. He gets his bearings, calms down, just tries to listen to his own breathing for a while.

int. tang-weller offices (tang 2)—buddy's office—day

Monday. Most of the support staff has been working all weekend. Buddy comes in to see Seth setting up their offices.

BUDDY

What do you think?

SETH

It's fine. You get a window, I get to work for someone who gets a window. What are you doing in here anyway? It's not even eight.

BUDDY

So I'm early.

SETH

How'd the date go with the realtor?

BUDDY

Fine, I guess.

SETH

Fine, huh? I thought she seemed nice. What happened?

BUDDY

What is this, Gay Confidante Day? Want me to hang on while you get your blow-dryer?

SETH

Hey, I don't give a shit, I'm just making conversation.

BUDDY

Well, it went fine but I'm not interested. So if she calls, just take a message. Say I'm out or busy and I'll get back to her.

SETH

And if she calls back?

BUDDY

Just keep taking messages. She'll figure it out.

SETH

That's what I like about working for you. The total freedom from hero worship. It's refreshing.

int. tang-weller (tang 2)—buddy's office—day

BUDDY

(on the phone)
Hey, you're the client, we'll sell anything. I'm just saying these new products aren't in sync with your brand positioning—

SETH

It's Jim on three. Urgent.

BUDDY

(into phone)
Yeah, look, I gotta call you back.
(punches line three)
Jim?

int. venice bar/restaurant—day

Abby's on her cell phone.

ABBY
No, it's Abby. Abby Janello. Hi.

int. office—day

Buddy looks into his outer office. Seth won't look at him, just keeps working.

BUDDY
Hey. How are you? I had a good time Friday night.

ABBY
Good, that's great. Look, I'm just across the street, I got some more keys from the seller to that closet downstairs. Why don't you let me buy you a drink? Celebrate your moving in. Bring Jim.

BUDDY
He's in a meeting and I don't drink.
(a beat as he decides)
Ten minutes.

He gets up and leaves, passing Seth in the outer office.

BUDDY
You don't know what you're messing with. It's not funny.

Seth watches him. He frowns. Maybe Buddy's right . . .

int. venice restaurant/bar—day

Buddy comes in, full of determination to tell her. He sees her at a table; she's working on some papers. He watches her a moment. Then she looks up, sees him. He approaches her table tensely; his mouth smiles but not his eyes.

ABBY

Hi. I ordered you a club soda. Is that okay?

BUDDY

Yeah. Great.

ABBY

My husband didn't drink either. Not once, not even champagne at our wedding.

BUDDY

Oh, I used to. I just don't anymore.

ABBY

Oh. AA?

BUDDY

Yeah. Six months.

ABBY

That's great. Meetings and everything?

BUDDY

When I have time.

ABBY

Oh. The keys. Here. That one's for the furnace room, he forgot that Thursday.
(she's at a loss; this isn't going well)
My uncle was in AA. But he was like a really bad drunk.

BUDDY

So was I.

ABBY

I'm sorry, I don't know why I said that.

BUDDY

But the drinking wasn't the worst. It was thinking I was such hot stuff, you know. I've always been one of those, you know. Born salesmen. A closer. A people person.

ABBY

Ew.

BUDDY

But I wasn't, not even close. It's like how everyone thinks they have a good sense of humor. Or good taste. Or they're good drivers. And there I'd be, driving along thinking, Hey, I'm a fucking great driver, and I'd happen to look in the rearview mirror and there'd be all these wrecked cars and bleeding people in the street and I'd be like, Wow, there's a lot of bad drivers in this neighborhood. That was me with people. And I'd like to think I've wised up a little, but I don't know.

Abby's face falls a little as she hears this.

ABBY

Yeah, I get it. You're bad with relationships.
(she stands up)
And as someone who's standing in the street ahead of you, thanks. I'll be getting on the sidewalk now.

She drinks her drink all at once, starts to leave.

BUDDY

Wait a minute, Abby.

ABBY

I . . . I took a shot, I'm sorry, I misread stuff. I'm just grateful about you throwing me the sale and all that and fine. Okay? Good-bye.

She leaves. Buddy tries really hard not to follow her.

ext. restaurant—sidewalk—day

Buddy runs up to Abby, who's walking, half running, to her car.

BUDDY

Abby! Wait! Please.

He grabs her arm. She stops, turns to him, angry.

ABBY

I'm not divorced, Buddy. My husband's dead, okay? He's been dead just a little over a year and I should have been honest with you because it's too soon for me and way too soon for my boys. Just leave me alone.

He follows her.

BUDDY

I'm sorry.

ABBY

Of course you are. Everyone's sorry and no one's to blame. Except most days I think exactly the opposite is true.
(she stops, fumbles in her purse)
Do you have a fucking cigarette?

BUDDY

No. Abby, please —

ABBY

(finding one, she lights it)
I'm sorry about lying, but you see what telling people does? They get like you, all nervous. And I liked thinking of Greg and me as divorced. Everyone's divorced. It feels like some kind of decision we made. It was up to us, instead of fate or bad luck or chance. Plane crash.

She starts walking again.

BUDDY

Come on, let's go back inside and start over—

ABBY

Don't be nice to me. Everyone's nice to widows. You're the first person who's been nice to me in a whole year who didn't know my husband died. But you don't have to be the nice guy here. In fact, it's better if you're not.

BUDDY

(stopping her)
Abby, please. I don't think I'm the nice guy, okay, that's what I was saying. But . . . I don't want you to go. I like being with you. I like you.

ABBY

What is it you want, Buddy? Just tell me.

And looking at her standing there trembling, Buddy suddenly realizes he can't bear to lose her. He tries to explain it to himself:

BUDDY

I don't know. Your company, I guess. The pleasure of your company. Your input on video rentals, maybe. I stand there for hours, you know, staring at them. Someone to say good night to. The last call of the day. I don't have a last call of the day, do you?

It sounds good to Abby.

                        ABBY

Don't feel sorry for me, Buddy. I'm happy. Widow happy, anyway. Widow-with-two-kids happy. You grade on a curve, I'm happy.

                        BUDDY

I don't feel sorry for you.

                        ABBY

Okay. Well.

She looks at him. He leans over and kisses her on the lips. She kisses back, gently.

                        ABBY

Then nothing with knives, snakes, or women who have to go undercover as hookers. The videos.

She smiles, gets into her car, drives off. Buddy watches her, scared and hopeful at the same time.

int. abby's kitchen— day

Abby and Donna are in the kitchen with SUE, a woman in her early thirties, thin but very pregnant. From the other room, we can hear a football game on TV. Abby and Donna are making a salad while Sue flips through the Multiple Listing Service book and eats carrots without pausing. Abby and Donna are at the sink, looking out the window at the backyard.

                        DONNA

Don't worry, I don't think he's getting bored, do you?

their pov—buddy

OUTSIDE, Buddy and a bespectacled, balding man (STEVE) are talking over a barbecue grill. Buddy catches her eye, widens his as if to say, "This guy's nuts."

back to scene

                    ABBY
(smiling at him)
Honey, it's a cookout. Of course he's bored. Aren't you?

Sue has joined them at the window.

                    SUE
Well, Steve can talk to anyone. I swear that's how he and Greg got most of their jobs. He's wonderful in a room, that's what his agent says.

                    ABBY
I guess I haven't been in that room yet.

Abby smiles as she sees Buddy feeding Buddy the dog hamburger off Steve's tray.

                    ABBY
Sue, do me a favor and see if you can round up the boys. Follow that little trail of wingless flies . . .

                    SUE
(leaving)
Boy, the way you talk about your kids. I hope that doesn't happen to me.

                        ABBY

I can't decide whether to get that baby some booties or a gun.

                        DONNA

Well? How far *has* it gone?

                        ABBY

Nowhere. He's a nice guy. Nothing special. Except, when you come to the table, he does that little halfway thing, you know, like he's going to stand up. I love that in guys. Greg did that.

Abby sees Donna watching her, gets busy.

ext. picnic table — day

Steve and Sue, Donna and her husband, JACK, Abby and Buddy, Scott and Joey. Scott has raced through his meal.

                        SCOTT

May I please be excused?

                        ABBY

CD-ROMS, but no AOL, okay? It costs money.

                        BUDDY

Hey, have you guys got *Where's Waldo?*

                        SCOTT

I'm eight, okay? Come on, Joey.

Joey hasn't finished. He looks at his mother.

                        ABBY

Take it. But no drinks on the desk.

The two boys disappear.

SUE

Let me help clear, Abby.

ABBY

No, no, let's take our time.

SUE

I don't know how you do it, working and then those two. Are you going to get help?

ABBY

Help with what?

SUE

Household help? When they settle?

ABBY

Well . . .

STEVE

Honey, we talked about this in the car, it's probably not, you know, smart to talk about the settlement while they're still negotiating.

SUE

Why, so you don't jinx it? It's going to happen, don't worry. Oh, that's what I meant to tell you, Abby. I heard on CNN what they're giving the guy who lost his wife and kids —

BUDDY

So, when's the baby due?

SUE

Hang on—and that's not even a loss of income thing because apparently when she was alive she didn't lift a finger. So you should do a lot better. It was between one and two, you know. They don't care, it's insurance money, the whole thing's a win-win for both sides.
(mouthing)
Million. One and two million.

ABBY

Okay, okay, fine, let me just answer your question. I'm not going to get household help, okay? It's not that big a house.

SUE

That was not his fault! You wanted to stay at home! Anyway, it doesn't have to stay small. You could put a wing on or go up, that's what I'd do, just blow out that roof.
(noticing the looks she's getting)
Well, I'm sorry. When you can afford anything you want I don't know what you're saving it for. I wish we could afford some of the nicer things in life for our baby.

ABBY

All you have to do is die, honey, you or your husband, all of a sudden and for no reason anyone can figure. Then you're dead and your little baby's rich and I don't have to listen to you ask about my fucking settlement every time I'm stupid enough to invite you over. That's what I call win-win.

int. living room—night

All the guests are gone. Abby's in the kitchen washing up. Buddy's waiting in the living room with Joey, watching TV. He hears the noise of a plane crash. . . . He gets up, goes over to a door leading off the living room.

int. janello house—office—night

Buddy sees Scott playing on the computer. Flight Simulator.

BUDDY

Whatcha doing, Scott?

SCOTT

Losing.

The SOUND of a plane crashing. Buddy comes closer.

BUDDY

Is it hard?

SCOTT

You can play. I'm done.

He gets up and leaves. Buddy knows he's been dissed. He looks around the room. It's been pretty much untouched since Greg's death. There's a picture of Greg and Abby on the wall; also Abby's glamour shots. From behind him in the doorway: *

ABBY

Sorry. He's still angry. With me, his dad, Joey. He teases him all the time. Says he's going to die if Joey doesn't do what he wants. Oh, and scared of flying. Can't watch any show where they fly. I'm going to take them on a little trip soon. You know. Fly someplace close so if they can't make it back we can rent a car and drive. Good idea?

BUDDY

That could work. Nice office.

ABBY

I'm the kitchen table type. This was Greg's. He and Steve used to work here. Nice computer, isn't it? It came two weeks before the accident, probably out of date already. He bought it to celebrate his play. He got this play on in Chicago. That's where he was, seeing his play.

Buddy's already seen a framed poster on the wall.

BUDDY

Uh-huh. *Lilacs in the Dooryard.*

ABBY

That wasn't the title I voted for. Who knows what a dooryard is?

Buddy runs his fingers along the computer keyboard.

ABBY

Steve bought Scott *Flight Simulator*, thinking it might help with the fear of flying. But he just likes to make it crash. He knows I hate it so it's hard to resist.
(as she tidies up the desk)
He was supposed to be on another flight. Even the paperwork in the beginning was wrong. That got me more than anything. You start thinking. The boys'd be getting ready for the bus and Donna would say, "Oh, I'm just going down there, I'll drop them off." And I'd like, I'd think, okay, which one is supposed to crash? Do I put them with Donna or keep them on the bus? Which one is doomed? Or is the whole thing supposed to happen tomorrow? Crazy, huh?

BUDDY

Can I ask you a personal question?

ABBY

I guess, yeah.

                             BUDDY
Do you have a good attorney for the case against the airline?

                              ABBY
I think so. It's a group thing, some of the other passengers' families. I've got his card here. Why?

She removes his business card from a bulletin board near the phone. Buddy looks at it.

                             BUDDY
Would you like me to check him out? Have our lawyers ask a few questions about him around town? For free.

                              ABBY
Oh, I get it. You're after my money.

                             BUDDY
It's not just the money. It's what the money can buy.

She smiles. He knows he maybe shouldn't, but he can't help it: he leans in, kisses her. She kisses him back. They kiss for a while—they sense Scott watching them in the doorway.

                             BUDDY
Okay. Thanks for the cookout.
(as he leaves)
Night, Scott.

We can HEAR him in the living room, saying good night to Joey. Then the front door closes. Abby looks at Scott. Suddenly:

                              ABBY
Boo!

He gives her a look of contempt, goes past her to the refrigerator. She grabs his arm, he pulls away, she tackles him, they end up on the floor wrestling. Joey comes in, sees them. A beat, then he piles on top . . .

ext. abby's house—night

About to get in his car, Buddy hears the screams and laughter from inside the house. It gets to him a little. That's the family he screwed up. Maybe still screwing up.

int. tang-weller (tang 2)—kitchen—day

Buddy looks like hell; he's had a sleepless night. As he pours himself a cup of coffee, Jim pops his head in.

>JIM
>
>Where've you been? I've been looking for you.

>BUDDY
>
>Here. I've been here. You see that creative brief Josh is pushing? Crap.

>JIM
>
>We had a meeting with Pat Dorian? The Canner Group?
>*(off his blank look)*
>You know. Publishing, broadcasting, advertising. They want to add us to their little family.

>BUDDY
>
>Are we up for adoption?

>JIM
>
>You tell me.

He opens a folder, gives Buddy a look at the top sheet. Buddy's impressed.

BUDDY

You're shitting me. This is real? When did this happen?

JIM

They were sniffing around when you were out in Palm Springs. They're interested. Fact, I had to run the real estate deal by them unofficially, see if it made sense to them.

BUDDY

When were you going tell me? I'm a fifth of the company here.

JIM

Look, nothing's going to happen without your approval. But personally, I approve of being made a millionaire. So should you. We'll bring this to the board Tuesday. What are you doing for lunch? Bring a calculator.

BUDDY

No, I got a thing—I gotta do a favor for a friend.

JIM

Tomorrow then. Great day, huh?

He smiles. Buddy tries to smile back.

int. reception area—lawyer offices—day

Buddy and Abby waiting.

ABBY

I'm not sure I want to separate us from the rest of the families.

BUDDY

You tell him what's been going on and let him give you his advice.

                         ABBY
I just think the guy we have now is kind of sleazy. I get the feeling he just wants to stick it to the airline. I have to keep telling him Greg's name.

                        BUDDY
Ben!

Buddy stands as he sees BEN MANDEL come into the reception area. Ben's fatherly but tough. Abby stands, too, nervous.

                        MANDEL
Buddy. Good to see you. This must be Mrs. Janello.

Abby smiles.

                         ABBY
Hi. It's nice of you to see us. I just—

                        MANDEL
I'm seeing *you*, Mrs. Janello, and you alone. I can't and won't ever disclose any of our conversations or decisions to any third party. As far as I'm concerned, Buddy's participation in this case is limited to the introduction we've just had.
(to Buddy)
If you'd like to wait—

                        BUDDY
Right. Call me at home when you're done. Good luck.

int. conference room

Mandel ushers Abby into the conference room. He closes the door. Pours her coffee, which is waiting for them. Finally:

MANDEL

So. Tell me about Greg Janello.

int. buddy's condo—night

Buddy opens the door. Abby is standing there, emotional, raw, barely in control.

ABBY

Fuck him. Just fuck him. Can I come in?

BUDDY

Ben? What did he say? Come in.

Abby enters, pacing furiously, tears on her cheeks.

ABBY

God, I'm so angry, so angry . . .

BUDDY

(alarmed)
Abby, please. Calm —

ABBY

Don't tell me to calm down. Everyone tells me to calm down! This is calm! This is as calm as you get when your husband blows up in midair.

Buddy's looking through the cabinets for something to offer her. Nothing.

BUDDY

I got water or Coke.

ABBY

(shaking her head)
Do you know what my mother said when Greg died? "When

God closes a door he opens a window." You believe that? Like that's a comfort. What's he doing fucking with my doors and windows anyway? He's got a whole universe, let him open his own doors and windows.

BUDDY

I had a girlfriend who used to say when God closes a door he turns on the gas. Here.

He hands her a glass of water.

ABBY

I don't even know why I'm doing this lawsuit. For the boys, I guess. We had some life insurance but . . . why shouldn't someone pay? Someone should pay. They don't even know what caused it . . .
(getting control of herself)
I'm sorry, have you got time for this? I couldn't go home.

BUDDY

Yeah, sure, sit down. Please.

ABBY

He wanted to know about Greg. Greg and the boys. Everything that happened, how I found out, how I told the boys, everything. I think he wanted me to cry or get angry so I'd make a good witness, so he could tell if I had the stomach for a fight.

BUDDY

So you're angry, that's not the worst thing —

ABBY

You think this is angry? This isn't angry, this is nothing. I don't let myself get angry. If I do, if I really let myself go there, I don't think I'll ever get back. And I have to get back, you know, for my boys. So I keep it here. Irritable. That's what losing someone does to you. You get cranky. Everything irritates the shit out of you. Like my mother. Even Donna, who's been so good. "Only the plane crashed, sweetie. You gotta bounce." That was Donna's take on it. And that's what I've been doing. Bouncing. It's like crashing except you get to do it again and again. Oh my God.

She's seen the TV, which is MUTED. It's playing some syndicated drama show.

ABBY

This is *Midnighter*. This was Greg's show.

BUDDY

Really, I was just flipping around—

ABBY

The one with the Vietnam vet—we got our new couch with this episode. God, what a stupid show. And he knew it, but to see him kind of talk himself into it . . . it used to depress me a little.

BUDDY

You gotta do that, you gotta psych yourself up for it.

ABBY

Don't do that— don't take his side. Now that he's dead everyone takes his side and I don't even recognize who they're talking about anymore.

BUDDY

Sorry.

ABBY

It's not that he wasn't a good man. He was, a really good man, but he wasn't perfect. He was a little tight with money, for one

thing, and he didn't want me to work. But the worst was—he wasn't this big confider, you know? He had secrets. Not other women or anything like that. But he kept things to himself. He liked knowing more than me. Little stupid things, like if he said yes to some invitation, he wouldn't tell me until the day before. Used to drive me crazy. He liked to surprise me, too. People who like to surprise you, I think it's a power thing, you know? Like, he'd give me surprise parties and I used to hate them, not the moment of the surprise or anything, but after the party, when you think, God, everything he said for the past two weeks was a lie. When he got on the flight—he called and said he was coming home the next day—he wanted to surprise me. So in the end I was right to hate his surprises.
(tearing up)
If I ever get angry, it's gonna be at him.

BUDDY

Abby . . .

ABBY

(in terrible distress)
I don't want to think of him as a good man. I want to blame him. Every time I hear someone say something good about him, it just makes me sick. It's so wrong to say this.

BUDDY

It's okay.

ABBY

Because I did love him. I really did.

BUDDY

I know, I know . . . Shhh.

Buddy puts his arms around her . . . then he kisses her; she kisses back. It's comforting at first, then more passionate, and then something they can't stop, and don't want to. And while they kiss and find each other, Greg's episode plays on, mute, behind them.

int. buddy's bedroom—night

Buddy and Abby make love.

later

Buddy's awake as Abby dresses behind him. She sits down to slip on her shoes.

>   ABBY
> I have to go. Donna has the kids.
>
>   BUDDY
> Abby, I—
>
>   ABBY
> I know what you're thinking. I just want you to know, this wasn't about Greg. I wish it were, because then I might not feel so guilty. But it wasn't. It was about you and me, not him. But I'd understand if . . . if it seems like I'm trying to work something out about him. So, you're off the hook, okay? You don't have to say another word.

This is Buddy's out. But as he watches Abby dress, vulnerable and touching, he can't—won't—take it.

>   BUDDY
> We still on for Thursday?

Abby is casual, hiding her relief.

                              ABBY
    Yeah, sure.

He grabs her arm, pulls her to him for a kiss. She leaves. Hold on Buddy. He looks at the clock: 9:00 P.M. He gets out of bed, pulls on his pants, looks for his keys.

int. buddy's outer office—night

Buddy, weary, worried, is walking down the corridor toward his office. As he turns the corner, he's surprised to see Seth in his outer office.

                              BUDDY
    What the hell are you doing here?

                              SETH
    I was over in production—their network crashed. Don't tell
    me you're working late.

                              BUDDY
    Lock the door when you leave.

He goes into his office. Seth watches him, aware that something's wrong. After a moment, he follows Buddy.

int. buddy's office—night

                              SETH
    I've been meaning to say, you know . . . anytime you want to
    pick up a meeting.
    (off Buddy's blank stare)
    You know. AA.

BUDDY

Oh yeah, sure.

SETH

You are going to meetings, aren't you?

BUDDY

God, I hate that you get to ask that question. I feel like a child molester. "Are you going to your aversion treatments? Still getting the little shocks when they show you the Garanimal underpants?" Yes, I'm going to meetings.

SETH

Okay, whatever. What's that?
(he looks at the storyboard)
Oh yeah. You approved this already.

BUDDY

I know.
(casually)
You know, I was supposed to be on that flight, the one that went down.

SETH

Duh.
(off Buddy's look)
We all know. The girl who comes around with the sandwiches at lunch knows. It's what they told us when you crashed and burned. It was the end of a speech that began, "You all might be wondering why we haven't fired his ass yet."

BUDDY

I gave my seat to someone else. I switched. Did you know that?

Seth instantly guesses how that's made Buddy feel.

SETH

Oh. Sorry.

BUDDY

That's not the worst part.
(with difficulty)
Abby's his wife. Widow.

For once Seth has no comeback.

BUDDY

She doesn't know. She just thinks I'm this nice guy. I've tried to warn her off. She doesn't believe me.

SETH

Maybe she'll believe *me*. You're an asshole. I could put on a slide show. How did this happen?

BUDDY

I felt guilty, like it was my fault—it *was* my fault—so I tracked her down to see if she was okay. I didn't even want to talk to her, but once I did, I just wanted to do her this favor and disappear. You know. To make amends. Step 5, right?

SETH

Step 9, and no.

BUDDY

Besides, she . . . you don't know her. She's a great person. I mean, courageous, funny, you know. A survivor.

SETH

We're all survivors. You're breathing, you're a survivor. When did that get to be such a great thing to be? What's next? "She's an eater." "She's a urinator."

• 99 •

BUDDY

She's not someone you get tired of. She's the first person I ever met, I'm more worried *she'll* get tired of *me*. I think back to before I met her and I'm like, fuck. How could that pass for a life, how could I get up every morning for that?

SETH

Buddy—

Buddy's suddenly angry.

BUDDY

It's not my fault the plane went down! It's not like I wanted him to die! It was just this tiny little thing that happened, me giving him my seat. Why should I let that keep me from this person? I've been punished, all right? I've paid. I'm not going to give this up, too.

SETH

If you don't tell her, every word that comes out of your mouth is a lie.

BUDDY

I haven't lied to her.

SETH

Tell her. If she's this great person, maybe it could work out.

BUDDY

"Oh yeah, I meant to tell you, I'm the reason your husband's dead. Chinese sound good?"

SETH

Get in your car and drive over there tonight.

                             BUDDY

(at his watch)
No, the kids might be up or—

                              SETH

There's kids?

Buddy nods. Seth looks at him like he's the loneliest guy on earth.

                              SETH

I'm sorry, man.

                             BUDDY

Just leave me alone, okay?

ext. miniature golf—day

Buddy, Abby, Scott, and Joey. Scott and Joey are playing up ahead.

                             BUDDY

(calling out)
Good shot, Scott.

Scott shrugs.

                             BUDDY

He doesn't like me.

                              ABBY

He doesn't like anybody. It's the age. I'm sorry about the sitter. And I couldn't ask Donna again.

                             BUDDY

No, it's fine.

(to Joey)
Here, Joey, let me help. Okay, now.

He stands at the cup, his feet angled so they'll direct the ball in. Joey putts; the ball goes into the hole. Joey drops the club, runs around to check. He yelps with delight.

JOEY

It went in!

BUDDY

Good.

SCOTT

He did it, not you. It doesn't count if you have help.

JOEY

Hey, Mom, can he come with us on the plane?

SCOTT

Shut up, Joey.

BUDDY

What plane?

ABBY

Our practice run, remember? Palm Springs.
(to Joey)
I'm sure Mr. Amaral is busy this weekend.

JOEY

Our daddy died in a plane.

BUDDY

I know.

SCOTT

I think it's dumb anyway.

ABBY

We're gonna do it, Scott, okay? We'll be back home before dinner.

The boys go on to the next tee.

ABBY

We had to drive to the funeral, Scott just wouldn't get on the plane. I don't want them to spend the rest of their lives afraid to fly. Greg'd hate his kids to live like that.

That does it for Buddy.

BUDDY

I'll go. I mean, it'll be fun.

ABBY

I promised them the water park out there, too.

BUDDY

What, they're scared of water, too? Fine.
(casually)
It's a big plane, right? I mean, that'll be easier for them.

ABBY

I think so . . .

int. airport—day

Sunday morning. Abby and the boys wait while Buddy talks to a female GATE ATTENDANT.

JOEY

What if the pilot drops dead?

SCOTT

There's a copilot, jerk.

ABBY

Don't say jerk.

JOEY

What if the copilot drops dead?

SCOTT

Then the stewardesses can drive the plane. They're all trained.

ABBY

Flight attendants.

buddy and the gate attendant

The Gate Attendant glances sympathetically at the Janellos.

GATE ATTENDANT

And this is their first trip since?

BUDDY

Yeah. And they're nervous. That's the mother and I'm a family friend.

GATE ATTENDANT

Is she scared, too?

BUDDY

No, she's fine.

                    GATE ATTENDANT
I had a friend on that flight. She used to work for us. Let me talk to them.

moments later

after Buddy has rejoined the family, they hear:

                    AIRLINES ANNOUNCER
(over the P.A. system)
Would the Gregory Janello family please report to gate 21 at this time?

Abby and the boys gather their things. She looks at Buddy.

                    ABBY
It feels funny, getting special treatment this way.

                    BUDDY
Yeah, but if it helps them . . .

He's looking green around the gills.

                    ABBY
Are you okay?

                    BUDDY
Yeah, sure. Let's go.

int. airplane—cockpit—day

The two boys are getting a tour from the CAPTAIN, who is showing them the instruments.

####### SCOTT

So who sits in that seat?

He points to the seat behind the copilot.

####### CAPTAIN

Sometimes there are two copilots.
(reading his mind)
Not passengers, though. Sorry.

####### SCOTT

It's okay.

####### CAPTAIN

But if you want to listen to me talking to the tower during takeoff, you put your headphones on number eleven, okay?

####### JOEY

Do you have a thing for your drinks?

####### CAPTAIN

Yup. Right here.

####### JOEY

I can have all the Coke I want for free, right? That's how planes work.

####### CAPTAIN

All you want.
(to Abby)
Well, that's about it. It's an honor having you on board, Ms. Janello. We'll give you a nice flight.

####### BUDDY

(whispering, ostensibly for the kids' sake)
Is there going to be much turbulence?

The Captain takes him in with a practiced eye. Abby notices it, too.

> CAPTAIN
>
> A boat on the water. Think of it that way. I mean, that's what you can tell the boys.

> BUDDY
>
> *(a memory)*
> Boat on the water, right. Okay, guys, let's settle in back there.

He and the kids leave. The Captain puts a hand on Abby's arm.

> CAPTAIN
>
> If you think it might help your friend, I can have him served a couple belts before we take off.

> ABBY
>
> He says he's not afraid of flying.

> CAPTAIN
>
> Uh-huh. Good luck.

int. plane—(stationary)—day

Abby and Buddy have facing aisle seats; the boys are between Abby and the window. They seem well occupied with watching the luggage being loaded on.

> ABBY
>
> You said you used to fly a lot. Why don't you anymore?

> BUDDY
>
> Oh, I don't know. No reason. Shhh!

He wants to watch the flight attendant demonstrate the safety belt, showing the safety card. His eyes are fastened on her as if she's explaining the meaning of life. Abby smiles, then her smile fades. Remembering Greg.

int. plane—(taking off)—day

The plane hurtles down the runway. The boys are craning to look out the window. Buddy is tense, tight. Abby reaches out for his hand, clasps it in hers. Buddy forces a smile.

BUDDY
It'll be fine. Happens a hundred times a day at this airport.

ABBY
Oh. I didn't know that.

BUDDY
Boys okay?

ABBY
They're fine.

BUDDY
Whoa. There we go.

There's a bump underneath them. Buddy tries to hide his alarm. Abby sees it. Casually:

ABBY
Is that the landing gear retracting?

Oh. That's what that was.

BUDDY

Yup. Hundred times a day.

Abby smiles.

ext. palm springs airport—day

The kids get out of the plane, cross the tarmac. Buddy is white but relieved . . . they head to the rental car desk.

ext. oasis water park—day

Buddy, Abby, Scott, and Joey, looking like any American family. Maybe happier than most.

On one ride with a height requirement, Buddy and Scott go together; Joey sulks at the gate with Abby.

Abby watches Buddy and Scott as they go by. She smiles and waves, then puts on her sunglasses to hide her eyes from Joey.

Abby puts sunscreen on three male faces; it only gets in Buddy's eyes. He makes a big deal about it for the boys' sake. Even Scott laughs.

ext. rancho mirage—day

Late afternoon. Despite the sunscreen, everyone's bright pink. The boys and Abby are asleep. Buddy passes a sign for the Desert Drug and Alcohol Center. It's a cloud on a perfect day.

int. airplane—day (in flight)

A little bumpy. Abby and the boys are fine. Buddy's white, his eyes closed. Abby notices, smiles. To distract him:

ABBY

Hey, you awake?

BUDDY

Oh yeah, sure. Dozing. You can really sleep on a plane.

ABBY

Boys, you ready?

JOEY

Yep. Where is it, Scott?

Scott reaches into the seat pocket in front of him, takes out a baseball hat.

JOEY

I want to do it. Okay, close your eyes and pick one.

There are slips of paper in the baseball cap. Joey shakes it up.

BUDDY

What is this?

SCOTT

You'll find out. Come on.

Buddy looks at Abby, who's smiling. He closes his eyes, reaches in, pulls out a slip of paper.

JOEY

Okay. You can open them.

SCOTT

Read it. We couldn't decide so it's up to you.

Buddy unfolds the piece of paper and reads what's on it.

BUDDY

Darth?

SCOTT

Yes! That was mine!

JOEY

It was my second choice, okay?

Buddy looks at Abby.

ABBY

The boys don't think the dog should have the same name as you.

BUDDY

(touched)
Oh. Well, thanks. That's great. And Darth's good, because he's black.

SCOTT

No, that's *your* new name.

Scott's delighted with his joke. Buddy laughs, a little uneasily. He's got to do something. He leans back in his seat so only Abby can hear him.

BUDDY

What are you doing tomorrow night?

ABBY

You tell me.

BUDDY

I have something to tell you. I don't think it's a big deal, but it's a little hard to say, so I got to tell you now that I mean to tell you, so you have to hold me to it.

ABBY

(only half-kidding)
If this is about how you've got a wife and kids in Playa del Rey . . .

BUDDY

No, no, it's nothing like that. You'll probably . . . it probably means nothing, I just want to tell you.

ABBY

Tell me now.

BUDDY

Tomorrow. Just . . . don't let me not tell you.

ABBY

Gee, this'll be a fun twenty-four hours.

BUDDY

It's nothing. Relax.

ABBY

Well, whatever it is . . . thanks for today.

BUDDY

Hey. Least I could do.

He turns to look out the window. Abby studies him, shrugs.

ext. abby's house— day

Abby pulls up to her house, as a woman at the front step is leaving a manila envelope on the mat. Abby stops the car, gets out.

ABBY

Can I help you?

The woman turns. We see it's Mimi, the woman Buddy picked up in the airport bar the night of the accident.

MIMI

(a little nervous)
Are you Mrs. Janello?

ABBY

Yes.

MIMI

Now that I'm here, I wish I'd just mailed this. I'm Mimi Praeger. Here.

She hands Abby the note she just wrote. Abby reads it, then looks at the manila envelope Mimi has in her hand.

ABBY

Please, come in.

int. abby's house—day

Abby and Mimi have just finished coffee. A videotape is on the table between them.

MIMI

. . . and I hadn't looked at it since then. But I was looking up a speech I'd given and there it was. I remembered the review for his play was in the Chicago paper, so I checked their archives, and . . . well. You probably don't even want to see it, but I thought, since I had this business trip . . .

                    ABBY
Thank you.

                    MIMI
I'm sorry. He seemed like a very nice man.

She stands as if to leave. Abby suddenly reaches out.

                    ABBY
Would you watch it with me? If I watch it now I can put it away.

                    MIMI
(not that she wants to)
All right.

Abby takes the tape, goes over to the VCR, puts it in, turns on the TV.

tv screen

We see the moments in the bar hours before Greg dies. Laughing, shouting. He comes on the screen. He shows his wedding ring. He's happy.

on abby

who watches, pain written on her face. And now something else—shock.

back to tv screen

which now shows Buddy:

BUDDY
(on the tape)
And Abby, whoever you are, forgive him, he did it for you.

On the tape we hear a boarding announcement for Flight 82.

BUDDY
(on the tape)
Ooops. That's me.

back to scene

MIMI
That's a guy I was with. I never got his last name. We were drinking. Cute, isn't he?

ABBY
What did he mean, "He did it for you."

MIMI
Your husband took a bump so he'd get this trip to Mexico for you. And then, just at the last minute, this guy gave him his seat so he could stay overnight . . .
(weakly)
We were flirting. Stupid.

ABBY
Fate, right?

MIMI
Yeah, I guess. Are you okay?

                    ABBY

I'm fine.

                    MIMI

Was it the right thing, bringing it?

                    ABBY

Yes, thank you.

They stand. Abby walks her to the door.

                    MIMI

Well . . .

                    ABBY

Thank you, Mimi.

Mimi nods, then goes. Abby closes the door. She goes back to the TV.

tv screen

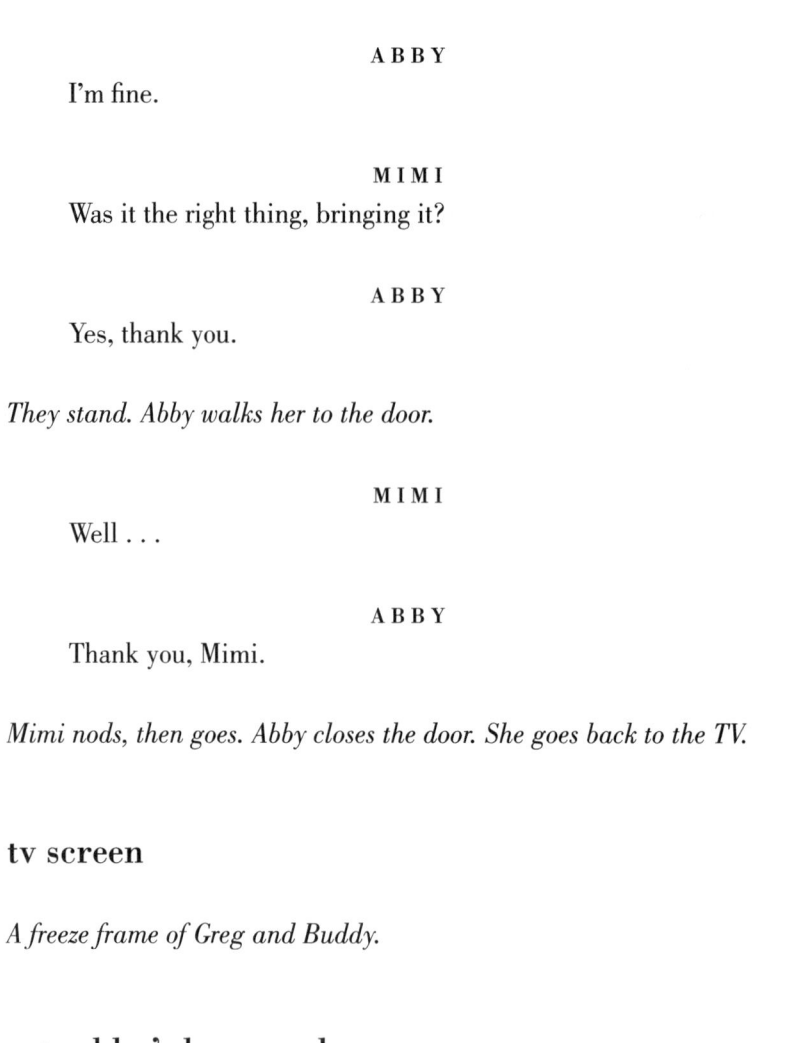

A freeze frame of Greg and Buddy.

ext. abby's house—day

After work. Buddy drives up, gets out.

int. abby's house—day

Joey's watching TV when Buddy knocks, enters. Darth (formerly Buddy) pounces on him.

                    BUDDY

Hey, Joey. Down, Darth, down.

                              JOEY

    Hey, Mr. Amaral.

                              BUDDY

    Abby!
    (to Joey)
    Where's your mom?

                              JOEY

    She's in the bathroom. She's been in there since *Rosie*.

                              BUDDY

    Jeez. Who was on *Rosie*?

                              JOEY

    Dunno.

int. hallway—night

Buddy taps on the door.

                              BUDDY

    Abby? You okay?

Scott shoulders past him on his way to the living room.

                              ABBY

    (from inside)
    I'll be out in a minute.

Buddy notices something about her tone, shrugs it off, goes back into:

int. living room—night

Scott and Joey are fighting over the remote to the TV.

                             BUDDY
                    (on his way to the kitchen)
                    Hey, hey, your mom's trying to relax.

                              JOEY
I was watching.

                             SCOTT
                    (re: a Hollywood Video tape on the
                    floor)
                    I gotta watch that, it's due tonight!

Joey kicks Scott and when Scott reacts, grabs the remote away from him. The VCR turns on. Scott pounces on Joey. Buddy intervenes, pulls Scott aside.

                             BUDDY
                    Hey, Scott. Don't hit him.

                             SCOTT
He bit me.

                             BUDDY
                    He's younger than you are. Joey, say you're sorry.

But Joey's looking at the screen. The volume's down low, but he's transfixed. Buddy looks from him to the TV.

tv screen

Greg is there, laughing and smiling.

back to scene

SCOTT

That's Dad!

JOEY

Hey, it's you!

— because Buddy is now on the screen. Buddy watches frozen. Suddenly, he jumps up, pushes eject, grabs the tape. Joey starts yelling.

JOEY

Hey! That's my dad! I want to see it!

Scott is smarter.

SCOTT

Did you know my dad? When was that taken?

BUDDY

I knew him a little. I . . . just once. We had . . .

He sees they are both looking past him. He turns to see Abby in the doorway in her robe. One look at her expression confirms she's seen the tape.

BUDDY

. . . a drink once.

ABBY

Boys, go to your rooms until I call you.

SCOTT

I have to watch this tape—

ABBY

Scott. Please.

Scott takes Joey out of the room. Abby waits until the door closes. A beat, then:

BUDDY

Who gave you this?

ABBY

Mimi. Mimi Praeger. Remember her?

BUDDY

Yeah. Abby, I . . . I've been wanting to tell you. That's the thing I said I was gonna tell you.

ABBY

That's a lie. Another lie.

BUDDY

I felt responsible. He took my place. And I wanted to make sure you were okay, you and the kids.

ABBY

Who the hell do you think you are? God? Some fucking angel, come to make sure the victims are alive and well? You lied to me.

BUDDY

I didn't expect to fall in love with you.

ABBY

Liar. Liar —

BUDDY

No, you know that's true—

ABBY

I want you out of this house. I don't want to talk to you again.

I don't want you to call. I don't want to hear your voice on my machine.

                    BUDDY

Give me a chance to explain.

                    ABBY

Didn't you hear me? Get out.

                    BUDDY

Abby—

                    ABBY

You son of a bitch. You lied to me. Get out!

Scott appears in the doorway.

                    SCOTT

Mom? What's wrong?

                    ABBY

Do you want me to say what you did in front of them? Because I'll do almost anything to get you out of here.

                    SCOTT

You better go, Mr. Amaral.

Buddy looks at Scott. He nods.

                    BUDDY

Okay, Scott. I think you're right.
(to Abby)
I'll call you.

                    ABBY

Joey!

(to Buddy)
Say good-bye to them. I don't want a guy just disappearing from their lives again.

Joey shows up at the doorway next to Scott.

ABBY
Mr. Amaral won't be coming around anymore.

BUDDY
Abby, please.

ABBY
You can leave, or you can say good-bye and leave.

Buddy takes a moment to think about it. He squats down on Joey's level.

BUDDY
I gotta go away. But I hope someday I can come back.

JOEY
Why?

BUDDY
I kept a secret from your mother.

JOEY
You can't tell a secret.

BUDDY
Then it wasn't a secret. It was just something I didn't want to tell her.

JOEY
Say you're sorry.

                              BUDDY

I am sorry, but . . .

                              SCOTT

It's okay, Joey.

Buddy straightens up, looks at Abby.

                              BUDDY

You have to let me call you.

                              ABBY

Get out. Before I tell them who you are.

                              BUDDY

Abby, please—

                              ABBY

Just stay away from us, okay? Do us the favor you didn't do Greg.

Buddy goes white. A beat, then he leaves.

                              JOEY

Dad's on TV, Mom.

                              SCOTT

She knows, you idiot.

int. buddy's condo — day (dawn)

Buddy looks like shit. He's been up all night trying to phone Abby. Finally he gets the announcement that the number has been changed and no new number is available.

int. restaurant—day

Abby and her lawyer, Ben Mandel, have just finished lunch.

> MANDEL
>
> I didn't know, Abby. I had no idea he was supposed to be on that flight.

> ABBY
>
> Okay. I had to ask. I thought you were friends.

> MANDEL
>
> Business.
> *(beat)*
> You say the employee at the gate knew they were switching?

> ABBY
>
> According to what Buddy told this woman. I don't want to talk about it anymore. You asked me why I was upset, I told you. Let me just sign the offer.

Mandel picks up the documents that were lying between them.

> MANDEL
>
> No, no, this is just a draft. I'll call you when the final comes in.

> ABBY
>
> Then why— oh, for God's sake.
> *(standing up)*
> I'm sorry, I'm grateful, Ben, really. You got us twice what they offered and that's going to help us get the hell out of here, move back home to Portland. But wrap it up quickly, okay? Thanks for lunch.

She leaves. Then he flips out his cell phone, makes a phone call.

MANDEL

(into phone)
Annie? Get me Travis at Infinity. Tell him I need some of their personnel files.

int. tang-weller (tang 2)—jim's office—day

Buddy enters, looking bad but not as bad as he will in a minute:

BUDDY

Jim? Seth says you wanted to see me?

He notices a lawyerly type, FRANK STEADMAN, sitting on the couch.

BUDDY

Hey, Frank. We being sued or something?
(to Jim)
What's going on?

JIM

We received a call this morning from Vince Gardia . . .

BUDDY

And . . .

JIM

Infinity Air, according to its marketing VP, is deciding today whether they'll be requiring our services in the future.

BUDDY

What? Why?

FRANK

Apparently they've received information that you coerced an Infinity employee to illegally board a passenger under your name onto Flight 82. You remember Flight 82? It's substantiated by their roster, which shows you listed on that flight.

BUDDY

We sorted that out a year ago, right after the accident. Some computer problem. There's a correct version of the roster in their system somewhere.

FRANK

Yes, there is. Do you know a Janice Guerrero?

BUDDY

I don't think so.

FRANK

She was fired six weeks after the accident for altering the flight roster. Removing your name, in fact, and adding the name of a—

BUDDY

(to prevent Jim from hearing his realtor's last name)
What's all this got to do with their account with us?

JIM

There's a suit against Infinity brought by the victims' families. You know Ben Mandel? He's got a piece of it. Anyway, they want to prove the airline didn't follow procedures. Even technicalities. So Infinity wants to make sure that if you are called to testify, you'll tell the court what you told us. That you didn't persuade this gate attendant to board you. Because if you don't, Infinity closes their account with us, we don't get acquired by Koerner, and nobody in this room gets rich.

Buddy thinks. Fuck.

                          BUDDY

But this woman's going to testify.

                          FRANK

Maybe. But she's not the most credible witness. Bitter ex-employee, ax to grind. Infinity's position is the roster screw-up's a harmless computer glitch, no big deal. And they want to know if you'd have a problem with that?

                          BUDDY

No. No problem.

                          FRANK

Good. You can expect to be subpoenaed. Naturally, we'll be your counsel. Jim.

He leaves. Jim, worried, watches Buddy.

                          JIM

That fucking crash, huh?

Buddy nods, tries to smile . . .

ext. janello house—street—day

Buddy has pulled up outside of Abby's house. He's got to see her. He takes a breath, gets out of his car, heads to the front door—and Scott comes out. Buddy stops. Scott comes toward him.

                          SCOTT

She's not home. Even if she was . . .

                          BUDDY

She doesn't want to see me.

• 127 •

SCOTT

Yeah.

BUDDY

I figured. Did she explain to you why she's mad at me?

SCOTT

You were with my dad in the airport and didn't tell her.

BUDDY

I wouldn't blame you if you were mad at me, too.

SCOTT

It's okay.

BUDDY

Okay. Good. Well, I guess I—

SCOTT

Did he say anything about Christmas trees?

BUDDY

What?

SCOTT

My dad. He was supposed to sell Christmas trees with me the next day. Maybe that's why he tried to get back on the plane that crashed. So I was wondering if he said anything about that.

Buddy has a chance to tell the truth. This isn't the time.

BUDDY

He didn't mention that to me. He just wanted to get back home as soon as he could. Everybody does when they're at the airport.

SCOTT

Because I didn't care if he sold those trees with me. I didn't want to, even. Everybody has fake ones anyway.

BUDDY

He said he had to get back home to work. I remember that. Nothing about the trees.

Something inside Scott eases, maybe for the first time since the accident.

SCOTT

Okay. Do you think I should tell my mom? Because maybe she thinks it's 'cause she yelled at him. Over the tree thing.

BUDDY

She might not believe me.
(not for his own sake)
You believe me, though, right?

SCOTT

Yeah.

BUDDY

Good. Joey okay?

SCOTT

Yeah. He's gonna forget you, you know. He practically doesn't remember Dad but I'm not allowed to say that to him anymore.

BUDDY

Yeah, well. You don't have to tell your mom I stopped by if you don't want.

SCOTT

I might leave it out. Just . . . I better.

                              BUDDY
    Okay. Well. See ya.

Scott gives him a little two-fingered salute, just like Greg did on page 13.

                              SCOTT
    Later.

This stops Buddy, but he smiles, goes to his car. Watches Scott staring at him as he leaves.

ext. buddy's condo building—night

Buddy comes home with a bag of groceries. Seth is at his front door.

                              SETH
    You forgot your ticket.

int. buddy's condo—night

Buddy's putting the groceries away; Seth is flipping through a folder.

                              SETH
    You're in the same hotel as Jim. He touched down about an
    hour ago with Frank.

                              BUDDY
    Okay, great.

                              SETH
    Phone list. Production estimate came in at five-three-zero.
    Josh says he'll handle the client call unless you want to take
    the heat. Everything else can wait. Oh, Ben Mandel called.
    "Sorry about the subpoena."

BUDDY

It's not his fault. And Abby . . . I guess you can't blame her for getting even.

SETH

She's not his client anymore. She settled. It was in the papers. Mandel glommed onto some other families.

BUDDY

She shouldn't have settled.

SETH

Yeah, why don't you call her? I'm sure she'd like your take on it.

BUDDY

You had dinner?

SETH

Are you asking me to dinner?

BUDDY

I'm asking if you had it.

SETH

Actually I've got plans with Adam. You want to come along? We'll sit you between us and you can pretend you're in prison.

Unthinkingly, Buddy takes out a liquor bottle from the Vendome bag. It's unopened, but . . .

SETH

What's that?

BUDDY

Oh come on, Seth. What are you going to do, give me a

lecture? Give me a break, the world's not exactly my fucking oyster lately.

       SETH

Don't let me stop you. In fact . . .
(sliding a glass over to Buddy)
It's not like it's part of my job to keep you sober.

       BUDDY

You got that right.

       SETH

Just like it's not your job to not disappoint me. Knock yourself out, man.

He leaves. Buddy looks at the bottle.

int. o'hare airport—infinity gate area— day

Late afternoon. Buddy exits the plane and sees the airport bar . . .

int. o'hare—infinity gate area—bar— day

Buddy looks at the cocktail table he, Greg, and Mimi shared a year and a half ago. For a brief moment, he sees Mimi and Greg—and himself—looking at him expectantly. He closes his eyes, opens them again. They're gone.

int. chicago hotel—day

Buddy's on the phone.

BUDDY
Oh, okay, fine. Jim, come on, go ahead and have dinner with them, I'm fine. Just don't tell me what you guys talk about, that'd be collusion. That's a joke. Call me when you get in. Room two-thirty-three.

He hangs up, flips on the news.

tv screen—local news

Too blonde, too many teeth, a reporter at the news desk with a blue-screen window behind her:

REPORTER
. . . earlier today in Kansas . . .

They roll some tape: a stone marker is unveiled . . .

REPORTER
. . . commemorating the two hundred and sixteen deaths on Infinity Flight 82 nearly eighteen months ago. Since then, Infinity, which began life as a commuter airline in 1979, has been plagued by lawsuits. Still, the upstart airline has successfully settled all but three of the lawsuits pending in the case, and its stock last week returned to its precrash levels for the first time. Wall Street's keeping an eye on the only case to reach the courts so far, which today entered its second week. The families of passengers Chris Hogan and Eloise Langan—

back to scene

Buddy flips the channel to something innocuous.

int. hotel coffee shop—night

Apparently Jim never called Buddy back. Buddy enters the hotel coffee shop near closing time—and sees Janice Guerrero at a table near the back. Buddy looks around, sees that no one is watching.

BUDDY

Janice?

Janice looks up at him. She's angry, and her eyes have dark circles under them.

JANICE

Oh. It's you. They called you.

BUDDY

You, too?

JANICE

Are you kidding? I'm an example of the sloppy, dollars-first attitude of Infinity. The plaintiffs love me— even though what they're saying is I killed their families.

BUDDY

You didn't kill anybody.

JANICE

Yeah, I've mentioned that. And they say if I'd done my job, that plane wouldn't have taken off.

BUDDY

No—

JANICE

Hey, I remember what happened. Don't you?

flashback: int. o'hare—night

Buddy and Janice are talking confidentially.

JANICE

I can't board him under your name.
(to Buddy)
Are you worried about the weather? It's just snow.

BUDDY

Janice, come on. If I don't board, you'll have to delay the flight until they take my bags off. This way . . . we just switch. You guys leave on time. It's fine. You want another half-hour delay?

JANICE

So I just didn't recognize you.

BUDDY

That's right. You never saw me.

JANICE

You owe me.

BUDDY

I'm back here next week.

back to scene (present time)

BUDDY

I should have been on that flight. I should be dead right now.

JANICE

Yeah, you should. Or at least just too fucking ashamed to come near me.

                                BUDDY
Janice, you—

                                JANICE
You could've called me, Buddy. You could have called me
once since the crash.

                                BUDDY
I didn't want to —I thought I was doing you a favor staying
away.

                                JANICE
Oh yeah, Mr. Big Guy, always doing people favors, always
making everything come out right. You think I'm so stupid I
don't know it's all about you? You think everyone you do one
of your favors for is that stupid?

She stands up and leaves.

ext. courthouse—day

Big crowds, cameras, reporters . . . Buddy and Frank Steadman, Tang-Weller's lawyer, pass a family member holding a photo sign: it's of Ron Wachter, the man Buddy talked to (see page 3). It stops Buddy when he sees it; then he goes inside.

int. corridor—day

Frank and Buddy show his subpoena to a BAILIFF, who shepherds them through the press stationed outside the courtroom. WE STAY ON A COURT TV REPORTER who's filing a live report.

                             TV REPORTER
Holly, Bill, I would say that was devastating testimony—
for those of you joining us this is day seven of the civil suit

against Infinity Airlines, and believe me, the tensions which have been running high since the suit began are likely to reach their peak today . . .

int. corridor—witness holding area—day

Buddy takes a seat on some benches in the hallway with the other witnesses. Frank's on his cell phone.

buddy's pov—other witnesses

A group of families are sitting together. It's obvious from their red-rimmed eyes they're the bereaved.

> TV REPORTER (V.O.)
> —the plaintiffs are the survivors of three passengers, two of whom, ironically, were seated across the aisle from each other, in seats 18B and 18C . . .

Buddy sees a commotion at the door to the courtroom. Suddenly cameras are snapping as Janice Guerrero exits the courtroom.

> REPORTER (V.O.)
> And Holly, here's today's principal witness, whose testimony about the boarding of Flight 82 exposed a disregard of safety that was extremely damaging to Infinity's case. Let's see if we can speak to her. Janice! Janice, please, are you sorry for what you did—

tv screen

with a COURT TV logo on it. Janice is being pushed through the crowd by her attorney. She shakes her head. "No comment," says her lawyer.

int. abby's house—kitchen—day

Abby's watching this on TV, riveted. In the month since we've seen her, she's taken up smoking again and called in sick most Mondays.

int. courtroom—day

Buddy is led in by the bailiff to the expectant court. Frank whispers a few words in his ear, then sits in one of the rows in the back, next to Jim. At the plaintiff's table sits Ben Mandel with two cocounsels. As he sits down on the stand, Buddy looks at the families. As he's sworn in—by the name of Robert Amaral—he sees Jim, who nods at Buddy, a "you-know-what-you-need-to-do" nod. Buddy nods back.

BUDDY

(taking the oath)
Yes, I do.

MANDEL

(rising)
Your Honor, this witness is affiliated with the defendant. We would like to treat him as a hostile witness.

JUDGE

Any objection? Proceed.

MANDEL

Mr. Amaral, you were scheduled to be a passenger on Fight 82, were you not?

BUDDY

Yes, I was.

MANDEL

In fact, when the plane went down, your name was on the first list of passengers, was it not?

BUDDY

That's correct.

MANDEL

But instead, a Mr. Greg Janello was in your seat, isn't that correct?

BUDDY

I believe so, yes.

MANDEL

You believe so?

BUDDY

I mean, yes, he was in my seat.

MANDEL

Do you know how Mr. Janello happened to be on that plane occupying your seat?

BUDDY

No, I uh . . . I don't know.

MANDEL

Excuse me?

BUDDY

I don't . . . I'm very confused about what happened that night.

MANDEL

You're not confused about having just taken an oath to tell the truth, are you?

INFINITY ATTORNEY
Objection, Your Honor. Badgering the witness.

MANDEL
I'll rephrase, Your Honor. Mr. Amaral, did you have a conversation that night with Mr. Janello?

BUDDY
I had a lot of conversations with a lot of people. Everything was delayed. It was a long time ago.

MANDEL
This is Mr. Janello.

Mandel holds up a picture of Greg Janello —half of the Greg-Abby photo Buddy saw in Greg's home office. Buddy stares at it, uncomfortable. He looks up, catches Jim and Frank watching him. He looks over at the Infinity lawyers.

MANDEL
Did you have a conversation with this man?

BUDDY
Yes.

MANDEL
And did you offer to switch boarding passes with him?

BUDDY
(he looks at Jim, then)
No.

Jim breathes out with relief. Then:

BUDDY
I just gave him mine. I didn't take his.

MANDEL

And when Ms. Guerrero recognized you at the gate?

BUDDY

I talked her into it.

MANDEL

By telling her if they didn't board you, or someone claiming to be you, they'd have to wait while they took your luggage out of the hold.

BUDDY

Basically, yeah.

MANDEL

Are you aware that airlines have to deplane the luggage of passengers who don't make the flight as an antiterrorism measure?

BUDDY

Yeah, in case someone checks a bomb or something and then doesn't get on the plane.

MANDEL

It's for safety, in other words.

BUDDY

Yes.

MANDEL

So this employee of Infinity disregarded a safety measure due to her desire to make the schedule.

INFINITY ATTORNEY

Objection! Argumentative!

                    JUDGE
Sustained—

                    BUDDY
—She just wanted to do me a favor.

                    MANDEL
No one's blaming you, Mr. Amaral. It wasn't your job to make sure the airline followed its own safety procedures, was it? No further questions—

                    BUDDY
He was scared, you know. I didn't remember that till later.

                    MANDEL
Excuse me?

int. airport—night (flashback)

Buddy and Greg in line at the Infinity gate.

                    GREG
You're not scared of flying, are you?

                    BUDDY
I'd rather be on a plane than anywhere. Safer than cars, you know.

                    GREG
You don't have any kids. They make cowards of you, children.

                    BUDDY
It's like a boat on the water.

GREG

Yeah, and boats never sink? "I know that I shall meet my fate/Somewhere among the clouds above." You know that one? Yeats.

BUDDY

Not the dooryard guy again.

GREG

"An Irish Airman Foresees His Death."

BUDDY

Kind of explains why I haven't run across it in the in-flight magazine.

GREG

This guy's this aristocrat. He guards people who can't be helped, and he fights people he doesn't hate, and since nothing means anything, why not live recklessly, you know? Bold guy, gambler. And I used to think when I was a kid, that's what you should shoot for. But instead I worry about cancer and drive-bys and bombs and de-icing.

BUDDY

Hey, when your number's up . . .

GREG

You gonna sleep with her?

BUDDY

Why not?

GREG

See, you got it. That whole "what me worry?" thing. I admire that.

back to scene in courtroom

BUDDY

But he was lying. He didn't admire it. He saw right through me. He knew I didn't care about shit, and that he did, and he had a wife and kids and a life that mattered, so much that he was scared of flying, and I had nothing and I thought for a second, Fuck you, pal.

Buddy's finally going to admit what he hasn't been able to till now.

BUDDY

I didn't know the plane was going to go down, okay? But I had this thought, which was, I hope you get four hours of turbulence, man, and maybe a tiny little sudden loss of altitude, and maybe you shit in your pants a little. Because he had what even I knew I wasn't ever going to have, and he knew it. And you don't wish those kind of people well. And then he died. And that's what I gotta carry.

There's a silence in the courtroom.

MANDEL

No further questions, Your Honor.

BUDDY

I'd just like to say I'm sorry.

But no one seems to be listening.

INFINITY ATTORNEY

No cross.

JUDGE

You're excused, Mr. Amaral.

BUDDY

Am I? Excused?

He smiles. "Excused." He gets out, walks out of the courtroom, past Frank's and the Infinity team's stony looks. Jim watches him, saddened.

int. janello house—kitchen—day

Abby watches this on the television, tears in her eyes. For Greg. And maybe for Buddy.

int. buddy's chicago hotel room—night

Buddy, packing, watching a wrap-up of the trial. In a surprise move, Infinity settled big with the plaintiffs—without admitting fault. We hold on him a moment, utterly defeated, down to zero. And yet, this is the first time he looks at peace. On the bed beside him is a paperback copy of Leaves of Grass *by Walt Whitman—Greg's "dooryard guy" . . .*

fade out:

fade in:

int. tang-weller (tang 2)—buddy's office—day

Buddy enters. Seth is there.

SETH
The word is you pretty much single-handedly sank Infinity.

BUDDY

Yeah, I noticed a chill on the way in.

SETH

Well, bundle up. Jim wants to see you.

BUDDY

Type this up for me, would you?

He hands Seth a letter. Seth reads it, looks up in surprise.

int. jim's office—day

Jim is reading the now freshly typed resignation letter.

JIM

I'm not accepting this. Infinity can hardly fire us because one of our team didn't commit perjury. Anyway, now they need us to handle the fallout from this settlement. Let's just sit tight.

BUDDY

Oh, they'll keep us on—but only if I go. They're waiting for you to make the move. Come on. It's for the best.

JIM

I won't let you resign.

BUDDY

Then fire me. Infinity likes that hardball stuff.

JIM

You're my friend. I'm not going to fire you.

Buddy takes a breath. He wishes he didn't have to say this:

                        BUDDY

You know the broker who handled this building? Abby?
She didn't find it. I told her about it. I threw her the sale.
She was someone I'd been seeing. I cost this company
$200,000. You don't need that, Jim. Fire me.

                         JIM

You lied to me?

                        BUDDY

Yeah. I'd do it again.

                         JIM

I wish you hadn't told me that, Buddy. I'd've fired you in
a week or so anyway.

                        BUDDY
              (not believing him)
Yeah, right, Jim. That's you. Take care.

He turns and leaves. Jim looks at the letter again, places it carefully in his "In" box.

int. buddy's office—night

Seth and Buddy are boxing up his office.

int. buddy's condo — day

Buddy stares into space.

int. seth's apartment—night

Seth and his boyfriend ADAM are making dinner. Buddy sits on a stool in the kitchen, watching.

####### SETH

I almost quit after you did. Then I thought, Shit, I don't even like the guy.

####### ADAM

Yeah, right.
(to Buddy)
You guys had me worried there for a while. The whole boss-secretary thing.

####### SETH

Hey. Boss-*assistant*.
(to Adam)
Look at him watching us. Like he's about to ask which one's the husband and which one's the wife.

####### BUDDY

You'll tell me when you're ready.

####### ADAM

Good. Then you can tell me.

####### SETH

How was the meeting?

####### BUDDY

Typical. Isn't it great we're not drinking? Incidentally, God rules.

####### SETH

Yeah, what's a nice guy like you doing in a place like that? Oh yeah, you're a fucking drunk.

ADAM

You know, we're thinking of a regional campaign where I work. We do interactive design, websites. It'd be mostly print and radio, but I could get you a meeting.

BUDDY

Hey, sure. Appreciate it.

SETH

Hand me that, would you?

He indicates a colander over by the wall phone. As Buddy reaches for it, he sees a calendar. On the calendar, next Saturday is circled with the word Abby. *Buddy looks at Seth.*

BUDDY

Is that Abby Janello?

SETH

Yeah. We got kind of friendly there while you were . . . whatever that was.

BUDDY

She ever mention me?

SETH

You want me to find out if she'll say yes if you ask her to the dance? Grow up, man. The boys survived, if you're interested. You want to eat or not?

He and Adam put dinner on the table. Buddy still has his eye on the calendar.

ext. rooftop parking lot—day

Late afternoon. Adam walks Buddy toward his car.

ADAM

That went well. He's not the easiest guy in the world.

BUDDY

I know the type. I was the type. Look, I can do mock-ups of what we talked about in two weeks. I gotta sub some of it out, but—

ADAM

Give us a proposal first. Bare bones, okay?

BUDDY

Yeah, sure. Thanks, Adam.

Adam hands him parking stickers. As Buddy sticks them on:

BUDDY

Listen, uh . . . when you guys see Abby tonight, would you mind just mentioning that I—

ADAM

Tonight? Oh, the calendar thing. That was for Seth. He went over there this morning to help her pack up.

BUDDY

What—

ADAM

She's moving back home—Portland, I think. You didn't hear that from me.

BUDDY

When, today?

> ADAM
>
> In fact, he and her friend, they're taking them to the airport now.

> BUDDY

Shit.

> ADAM
>
> *(after a beat)*
> Nine-thirty. LAX. You didn't hear that from me, too.

> BUDDY

Thanks, Adam—

> ADAM

Hey, Buddy? Seth likes the cheap lots.

ext. lax—parking lot c—night

Buddy pulls into the remote parking lot and drives down the aisles, looking for Abby and Seth. He sees them, and Donna, behind him, but now a shuttle bus and car are blocking him. He gets out of the car, starts running, calling Abby's name.

abby, seth, and donna

are pushing some trolleys loaded with luggage. Joey and Scott are ahead of them. Abby hears Buddy shouting her name. She turns, sees him, then looks at Donna.

> DONNA

I didn't tell him.

> SETH

Fuck. Adam.

BUDDY

Abby! Abby!

Now Scott and Joey have stopped, are looking back at Abby, Seth, and Donna— and beyond them, Buddy.

ABBY

(to Scott and Joey)
Go on, keep going.

SETH

He'll just get on the plane. He'll be puking with fear, but it's possible. I'll wait with the boys.

ABBY

No, wait, wait—

DONNA

You want me to stay, I'll stay.
(a look at her, then to Joey and Scott)
Guys! Wait up!

They leave with the luggage. Abby breathes in, turns to face Buddy, who arrives panting, his face damp with sweat.

BUDDY

Thank you. Thanks.

He's out of breath. He leans against a nearby car.

ABBY

Are you all right?

BUDDY

Yeah, yeah. I . . . you look . . . beautiful.

ABBY

It's the jet exhaust. Filters the light. Well. We're leaving for Portland.

BUDDY

I know. Adam told . . . I didn't hear it from Adam.

ABBY

I didn't want to see you again.

BUDDY

I know, I don't blame you—

ABBY

But I did. On TV. At the trial. I heard what you said about Greg.

BUDDY

I don't know why I said that—

ABBY

Maybe because it was true. Unless that's not a reason for you.

BUDDY

No, it is. Abby, I just—

ABBY

Hey. I got a marriage proposal. From Steve—Greg's old partner, remember him? He came over one night a month after Sue had the baby. I kicked him out and he called the next day and said it was the postpartum depression, and I said, She'll snap out of it, and he said, No, *my* postpartum depression.
(beat; this kills her:)

I don't want to hear anything from you, Buddy. I just don't because it's no good.

BUDDY

I don't expect you to forgive me. I don't deserve it. But who deserves anything they get, you know? You didn't deserve what you got, or the boys, or Greg. So maybe being forgiven will be what I get and don't deserve.

ABBY

I've forgiven you, Buddy.

BUDDY

I thought maybe we could talk someday. That's what was in my letters. Maybe today's not good, or soon, but . . .
(he can't finish; simply:)
I want to see you, Abby. Not seeing you is harder than anything.
(trying to joke)
You know what that does to a person. Makes you irritable.

ABBY

Yeah, I miss you, Buddy, and I miss him, and sometimes I can't tell the two feelings apart. And it makes me so angry. Let me ask you something, and if you lie to me I'll know. Are you sorry you didn't get on that plane?

BUDDY

(after a beat)
No. I'm sorry, but I'm glad I'm alive.

ABBY

And nobody blames you for that. But ask *me* the question. Am I sorry you didn't get on the plane? Whatever I answer, yes or no, it feels like I'm doing something wrong to someone I . . . to both of you, you and Greg. Being with you is like making a choice.

                            BUDDY

You don't have that choice, about whether he lives or dies.
Neither do I. We've got other choices.

                             ABBY

What am I supposed to do? Pretend we've never met before?
You never met Greg, you weren't the one who —

                            BUDDY

No, I'm the guy who *lived* instead of him. That's who you'd
be talking to.

*Inside Abby something clicks into place. She looks at him and quietly
makes her choice. While Buddy waits to be told, an airplane makes
a deafening noise from the nearby runway as it prepares for takeoff.
She turns to look at it. So does he.*

                             ABBY

This is the scary part. Now, right before it takes off. Because
it just seems so . . . unlikely.

                            BUDDY

You're not scared of flying.

                             ABBY

I'm not talking about flying.

*She looks at him, and then again at the plane approaching. Together
they stand together and watch the plane coming closer and then lifting
away from the ground, toward them, and over their heads.*

*From behind we see them standing, looking up at the plane. Then
Buddy reaches for her hand, and she lets him take it, that's all, and
they still stand there, watching.*

*And then they turn, toward us, and Abby's smiling and brushing
something from her face and raising her hand to wave to her kids, and*

Buddy picks up her bag, not letting her go, and then they're both past us and we're following behind them, and beyond them WE SEE Scott and Joey begin to walk and then run toward them and US, and just as they reach Abby and Buddy, WE GO UP and over them, and then OUT to the sky, where the plane is only lights now, among hundreds of lights, and we hang there a moment and then . . .

fade out:

THE END